THE LEADER WITHIN

7 STEPS TO ASCENSION LEADERSHIP AND INTUITION IN BUSINESS

COURTNEY JONES

WHY NOT HAVE COURTNEY JONES AS A GUEST SPEAKER ON YOUR NEXT PODCAST OR AT YOUR NEXT SEMINAR OR EVENT?

LEADERSHIP ASCENSION ACADEMY – COURTNEY JONES

Email: hello@theleader-within.com
Website: www.theleader-within.com | www.leadershipascensionacademy.com

This is a callout to all those who consider themselves an 'undercover intuitive' in their workplace, life, business and in their role as a Leader.

Courtney is a self-confessed 'undercover' intuitive. Alongside her private coaching practice, she continues to work with government and not-for-profit (NFP) organizations on strategic projects.

Her passion for Positive Psychology and Energy Medicine has led her to a unique approach to leadership that empowers her clients with her Ascension Leadership Model to integrate intuition into their corporate and personal lives.

BOOKS BY COURTNEY JONES

THE LEADER WITHIN
7 Steps to Ascension Leadership and Intuition in Business

This book is for all women who feel called to lead with their hearts and create positive change in the world. It is for those who know there is a compassionate way to do business that uplifts the communities they serve.

ONLINE PROGRAM BY COURTNEY JONES
Advanced Certificate in Ascension Leadership
Ascension Leadership Coaching Certification

MENTORING GROUP WITH COURTNEY JONES
Group and individual mentoring opportunities with Courtney are available by application.

www.theleader-within.com
www.leadershipascensionacademy.com

THE LEADER WITHIN

7 STEPS TO ASCENSION LEADERSHIP AND INTUITION IN BUSINESS

COURTNEY JONES

The Potentialist
by *Maggie White*

Mind Potential Publishing

Copyright © 2020 Courtney Jones

ALL RIGHTS RESERVED. No part of this book may be reproduced or transmitted in any form whatsoever, electronic, or mechanical, including photocopying, recording, or by any informational storage or retrieval system without the expressed written permission from the author and publisher.

Author: Courtney Jones
Title: The Leader Within
ISBN Paperback: 978-1-922-380-24-1
ISBN Kindle: 978-1-922380-26-5

Category: Business | Self Help Techniques

Publisher: Mind Potential Publishing
Division of Mind Design Centre Pty Ltd,
PO Box 6094, Maroochydore BC Queensland, Australia, 4558.
International Ph: +61 405 138 567
Australia Ph: 1300 664 544
www.thepotentialist.com | www.theleader-within.com

Cover design by NGirl Design | www.ngirldesign.com.au

 A catalogue record for this book is available from the National Library of Australia

---

LIMITS OF LIABILITY | DISCLAIMER OF WARRANTY: The author and publisher of this book have used their best efforts in preparing this material and they disclaim any warranties, (expressed or implied) for any particular purpose. The information presented in this publication is compiled from sources believed to be accurate at the time of printing, however the publisher assumes no responsibility for omissions or errors. The author and publisher shall not be held liable for any loss or other damages, including, but not limited to incidental, consequential, or any other. This publication is not intended to replace or substitute medical or professional advice, the author and publisher disclaim any liability, loss or risk incurred as a direct or indirect consequence of the use of any content.

Mind Potential Publishing bears no responsibility for the accuracy of the information provided as either online or offline links contained in this publication. The use of links to websites does not constitute an endorsement by the publisher. The publisher assumes no liability for content or opinion expressed by the author. Opinions expressed by the Author do not represent the opinion of Mind Potential Publishing or Mind Design Centre Pty Ltd.

Printed in Australia

DEDICATION

To all the inspiring women I have worked with over the years.

Thank you for being willing to step up and become conscious creators. For having the courage to face your greatest fears and heal your deepest wounds. Thank you for trusting me to guide you in your transformation and in turn showing me how to joyfully live my purpose. It is only through our work together that the Ascension Leadership Model has been born. Through the insight and awareness gained as we grew and learned together, this model has a profound intent that will continue to serve as a guide for others like you, who choose to step into their creatorship.

CONTENTS

A Word by Dr. Sue Morter		1
A Word by Margot Cairnes		3
Introduction		5
Chapter 1:	The Ascension Leadership Model	17
Chapter 2:	The Leader Within - Your Intuitive Self	27
Chapter 3:	Where Are You Now – A Baseline for the Ascending Leader	47
Chapter 4:	Liberate the Leader Within	67
Chapter 5:	Activate Your Energy Through the Chakra System	79
Chapter 6:	Your Unlimited Leadership Potential	109
Chapter 7:	Ascend Beyond Now – Stepping into the 12 Chakra System	125
The Leader Within		143
Glossary		146
Acknowledgments		148
References and Recommended Reading		149
Meet the Contributors		151
Meet the Author		161
Works by Courtney Jones		163
Credits for Chapter Images		164
What Others Have to Say		165

A WORD FROM
DR SUE MORTER ABOUT *THE LEADER WITHIN*

(This is an excerpt from the Foreword written by Dr Sue Morter. Please refer to 'Meet the Contributors' to read Dr. Sue's valuable full commentary.)

As the world around us continues to change at a rapid rate, the need for Conscious Leadership is greater than ever. The change we are in need of will take courageous women to step up and into their inner wisdom and to embrace their personal power to become ascended leaders.

Throughout my three decades of helping people access their creative wisdom, I have seen more and more evidence of how working with energy and intuition can spark unprecedented personal growth. That step allows leaders to tap into creativity, power, health and compassion to nurture themselves and their relationships. So, too, does it enable them to empower people around them and the community in which they live to activate their potential.

Using high frequency energy patterns, I have worked with people from all walks of life to assist them in elevating their consciousness into life mastery. The Ascension Leadership Model from Courtney Jones speaks closely to an increasingly loud inner calling. The book provides a pathway for coming to know yourself, by unravelling self-imposed limitations that have denied people their true joy and meaning.

This book and Courtney's *Ascension Leadership Model* elegantly combines cognitive, energetic and spiritual techniques to provide a strong foundation for creating our life experiences and achieving fulfilment on every level. The bridge between science and spirituality has been firmly established. Finally, the field of Quantum physics is proving age-old philosophies of energy healing and connectedness with the environment, bringing forward undeniable evidence of the vibrational reality of life. Allopathic health practitioners no longer dismiss energy as a contributing factor to health and healing and are finding more ways to integrate this aspect into their work.

This book and Courtney's Ascension Leadership Model elegantly combines cognitive, energetic and spiritual techniques to provide a strong foundation for creating our life experiences and achieving fulfilment on every level.

I am pleased to see Courtney's work offered to the world at a time when it has never been more needed. An essential, fresh approach to the subject of leadership, there is no doubt this book will empower, uplift, and serve as a catalyst for significant positive change.

Dr. Sue Morter
International Speaker, Author and Quantum Field Visionary
Founder and CEO of Morter Institute for Bioenergetic Medicine

A WORD FROM
MARGOT CAIRNES ABOUT *THE LEADER WITHIN*

(This is an excerpt from the Foreword written by Margot Cairnes. Please refer to 'Meet the Contributors' to read Margot's valuable full commentary.)

Courtney Jones reminds us of the Dalai Lama's assertion that "The world will be saved by the western woman." The world needs saving.

The UN tells us that in February 2019 only 24.3 per cent of all national parliamentarians were women and that as of June 2019, only 11 women were serving as a Head of State and only 12 were serving as a Head of Government. As there are 195 countries in the world this means that only 11% of countries have a woman at the helm.

Figures in the business world are even worse - only 6% of Fortune 500 companies are headed by women!

Women such as Jacinda Ardern, Prime Minister of New Zealand and Erna Solberg, Prime Minister of Norway show us that leaders can be compassionate, wise and operate from higher level values.

Figures in the business world are even worse - only 6% of Fortune 500 companies are headed by women!

This wonderful book, *The Leader Within*, is a practical manual for women who want to step up as leaders. It is filled with wonderful tools, insights and models to help you live life to the fullest and bring those about whom you care, along with you on the journey.

A WORD FROM MARGOT CAIRNES ABOUT THE LEADER WITHIN

We need structural change. To get such change we will need to lift our levels of consciousness and subsequently, our values. In this book Courtney Jones gives us practical tools to grow as human beings; to be more alive, more aware and more purposeful.

> *This book contributes to us becoming the kind of leaders we will need to be to bring about the change that needs to happen.*

Women can save the world. This book contributes to us becoming the kind of leaders we will need to be to bring about the change that needs to happen.

Margot Cairnes
International Leadership Strategist
The American Biographical Institute calls Margot *"One of the Great Minds of the 21st Century."*

INTRODUCTION

"We think, mistakenly, that success is a result of the amount of time we put in at work, instead of the quality of time we put in." **Arianna Huffington**

When Albert Einstein said *"the only real valuable thing is intuition"* the people around him must have been a little surprised. A man well known for his ability to analyze and think critically, someone so renowned for his mental genius, and here he was espousing the value of intuition?

On the surface, it may not have appeared to make any sense, but, in truth, Einstein was giving us the key to a perfect and complete way of seeing and understanding the world around us.

- Intuition and logical thinking are often seen in great contrast, and in business we are encouraged to use our heads, be logical and think strategically.

- Taking a left-brain approach to decision making and problem solving is considered the safest and most professional way to conduct business, it is just the way things are done.

But is this approach flexible enough to meet the challenges of a shifting global economy? Is it agile enough to radically change a business' direction while meeting the financial, social and environmental expectations of today?

INTRODUCTION

This book provides a model to transcend rigid ways of thinking. A model that is underpinned by a strong intuitive sense and an ability to understand issues from a broader perspective. It shows you how to identify the patterns and themes that hold the keys to creative solutions and to recognize the subtleties that reveal the truth in any situation.

> *Once you become aware that thinking and knowing is not just in your brain or head, and you learn to tune in to your body and use its subtle signals, you create a strong mind-body connection to support your cognitive thinking.*

When you recognize the way your brain and body processes information when making decisions or facing challenges, you can identify whether your world view and 'mode of perception' needs to be upgraded or more flexible.

Once you become aware that thinking and knowing is not just in your brain or head, and you learn to tune in to your body and use its subtle signals, you create a strong mind-body connection to support your cognitive thinking. Through this you increase the positive impacts of your decisions.

The way you think is an important factor in your ability to make decisions and be successful. Left-brain thinking on its own is an inefficient use of energy. Switching to an intuitive integrated approach enables you to unify your skills and experience in your specific field of expertise. You can coalesce that experience into an unconscious process that supports you to not only make a decision, but instantly know and trust that decision.

Intuition is not about being 'airy fairy' or giving responsibility to an outside unknown source. It is no longer seen as 'woo woo', 'out there' stuff for hippies and dreamers.

Intuition is inner listening

Intuition is tuning in and establishing a strong reliable process for deciphering your body's signals and interpreting the energy around you.

- Intuition is based on all your experiences that are stored at an unconscious level.
- Intuition is an inner source that you can access at any time and use as a font for information and insight beyond what is apparent at the cognitive data-driven level.
- Being intuitive in business is fast becoming known as the new way to lead and innovate.
- Many CEOs and managers across the globe are currently learning how to be more intuitive.

Rachel Zoe

Rachel is a globally renowned fashion designer, stylist and businesswoman. She said in her interview for the book *Game Changers*, "I always use my intuition in business, if something doesn't feel right, I don't do it."

Richard Branson

Richard is quoted as saying, "I've always relied on instinct when it comes to calculating risks, putting trust in people and making important business decisions. There are some things that can't be summed up in a statistic, and this is when you need to use a bit of intuition."

Ways of doing business

The traditional way of doing business is shifting. Evidence-based cognitive models are evolving to support a structured approach to learning intuitive decision-making skills.

INTRODUCTION

> *Where it gets interesting is when you come to understand that thinking is not just in your head.*

All of this is building our understanding of intuition and furthering our ability to map decision-making strategies and styles. Once mapped, these styles can be embedded into corporate cultures and training packages for the next generation of leaders.

This book explores the currently accepted epistemology and provides a way of understanding your unique cognitive processes for decision making. Where it gets interesting is when you come to understand that thinking is not just in your head.

> Throughout this book you will come to realize that your entire body is your mind, and your 'bodymind' is far more intelligent and creative than you have been led to believe.

All modes of thinking, all beliefs, values systems and ideas carry an energetic resonance. Understanding bodymind communication is the key to connecting with your intuition and becoming familiar with the energetic resonance of the circumstances around you and the potential outcomes of your decisions.

The Ascension Leadership Model

This model is rooted in the knowing that everything is energy. When you become aware of and sensitive to energy, you will begin to see how you can consciously shift and focus your energy and work with the dynamics of the energetic influences around you.

The Ascension Leadership Model shows you how to identify areas of thinking where you may be limited by values or ideas that are no longer relevant to you. It provides a protocol for resolving these values and transcending to a new level of perception. Coupled with a process for clearing blockages from the body's energy centers or chakras, this model is the pathway to personal evolution and a higher level of consciousness as a leader.

It is that higher level of consciousness that is creating so much good in the world today.

There is far more out there to be optimistic about than we care to or are encouraged to recognize. Traditionally the media focuses on the negative, the drama, the tragic and the unjust. The human brain by design is geared to look for the negatives — the threats or dangers that challenge our survival. But we no longer live in a 'might be eaten by a tiger' world. We have overcome these threats; we have technology and education and health care and infrastructure. However, the human brain in some respects has remained primitive.

Being an effective leader and inspiring others, demands a different perspective. It is a requirement that you move beyond your current limitations and change the things you look for in the world. If you are always on the lookout for danger and gloom, you will only see danger and gloom. When you seek out the positives, the advances in technology, the new-thought movements, the strategies that provide equity and equality — these positive aspects will become more and more present and more available to you as tools for problem solving and leading.

INTRODUCTION

Who is this for?

This book is for professional women who sense there's a better way, a more effective way, to get great results that provide far more than just bottom line, KPI, toe the line outcomes.

You know deep down, there's more

- More you can do for your staff.
- More you can do for your business or organization.
- More you can do for your community.
- More you can do for your career and yourself.

It doesn't have to mean more of your time, more of your energy, more stress or more of the same. This book is for those of you who have a deep knowledge and understanding of your core business, or industry, backed by years of experience. Importantly, you have a deeper desire to purposefully use that experience to create greater meaning in your life and a larger contribution to those around you.

Your Current Leadership Dilemma

If just one or two aspects of this work-life scenario are familiar then keep reading, this is definitely the book for you!

It's 7.30pm and you're still at your desk. You've spent the day solving problems for everyone else and you haven't even started on your own to do list. Your inbox is crammed with questions and demands and there are deadlines everywhere.

- You need to sign off on a few things, but you're paralyzed.
- You feel like you're forever fighting for your opinion or justifying your decisions so you're second guessing the decision and reviewing all the details.
- Your head begins to ache (or has it been aching all day, but you just haven't had time to notice?)
- Your neck is sore, and you just realized you skipped lunch. Just like you did yesterday and the day before and the day before that.
- At this point you're just trying to keep your head above water.
- You're functioning on autopilot, watching the same scenarios play out each day, go to work, do the task (pray it's good enough to please everyone) go home —rinse and repeat the next day.
- Yes, you've got respect from your peers and friends, a steady income, but you've got this feeling, a niggle, and perhaps a little hum of anxiety too.
- You try to ignore all that because there is so much to do.
- But the niggle blossoms into full-blown anxiety. You're overwhelmed, frustrated, and perhaps even have a sense of defeat.

Moving Beyond

How do you move beyond the stress and madness of trying to get it right and on time, every time? How do you reconnect with the passion and enthusiasm you once had for the job or the industry, when it is sucked out of you by the weight of expectation? Why are you so mentally exhausted, physically drained and feeling a little adrift?

INTRODUCTION

The path to find me

In this lifetime I have been fascinated to witness very different leadership and communication styles. Extremely different ways of doing business.

I have worked for government organizations and not-for-profit organizations (NFPs), I've been self-employed, I've been a clinical hypnotherapist and a life coach. In each different position and workplace, I have tried to look back and compare, to see if I can identify which way of leading was more effective. Which way got better results, which approach created a happier experience for staff and a healthy corporate culture. As someone who was often on a short-term contract, I was mindful to take the perspective of an outsider looking in. I consciously observed each culture without getting caught up in the 'group think' or inherited perspectives of the people who had 'been around for a while.'

In one government department I noticed we would often be told one thing, but see another thing demonstrated by the managers. The apparent conflict with the corporate values made it challenging to figure out the best approach to moving projects ahead or developing business cases and strategic plans.

This experience drove my desire to find a way of improving my communication to get a clear picture of what was being communicated to us from the top down. I read management books (melting icebergs, stolen cheese, world cafes, fish markets) and countless articles about leadership styles, but still didn't find clarity.

I don't believe in fate as it is commonly understood but I do believe things happen as they should, which is different to 'everything happens for a reason,'

By an awesome twist of fate (I don't believe in fate as it is commonly understood but I do believe things happen as they should, which is different to 'everything happens for a reason,' (I'll talk about this concept later) I began studying Neuro Linguistic Programming (NLP).

This was in 2015 when I was working for a large state government department, managing multiple stakeholder groups in the delivery of road safety projects. NLP gave me the tools to recognize motivating factors and underlying values when talking with these stakeholders. It revealed the thought processes and decision-making strategies that could be reliably appealed to, to facilitate clearer communications and greater collaboration.

By this time, I had also begun supporting management clients as a wellness practitioner and life coach. I began to see patterns of language that pointed to emotional disharmony. These gave me clues as to how to lead a person through a process of self-discovery so they could resolve personal issues and gain new perspectives.

This led me to a deeper understanding of the mind-body connection and into further studies to educate others in these fields.

This led me to a deeper understanding of the mind-body connection and into further studies to educate others in these fields.

The clients I worked with confirmed my beliefs that many of us are ready to acknowledge our agency and ability to self-heal and resolve personal problems. There is a growing body of evidence and social acceptance for cognitive therapies and working with unconscious patterns. I now mentor clients to move beyond their current limitations and see themselves as being capable of achieving their highest potential.

Often my clients are highly skilled and accomplished in their field but have an underlying sense they have more to offer, and feel there is some unknown, unseen obstacle blocking them. I have continued my studies in positive psychology, behaviorism, energy medicine, counseling and metaphysics. The underlying theme through my studies is to support a person to resolve life challenges with the understanding that every connection we make is influenced by an energetic vibration that either supports or hinders growth and change. The way in which a person perceives themselves and the world in which they live is deeply influenced by that energy.

What to expect

Within these pages you'll learn tools and strategies to recognize the context and energetic influence around you and take the hard work out of your day-to-day tasks to rediscover inspiration and flow in your work. Through reading this book you will:

- Learn about your current thinking and how to evolve to new levels and develop your personal process to confidently make decisions that benefit your business or career.

- Discover what sets you apart as an innovative leader with integrity and a record of success.

- Learn how to enter a state of flow and connection that makes decision-making easy by using your body as a tool to find the answer to any question you may have.

- Explore the concepts of energy and intuition and how to apply this in the real world as a leader and key person of influence within your field.

- I will give you an outline of the codes for living that exist across humanity at this time so you can identify your key values and modes of perception to assess your internal alignment with the decisions and the purpose of your work.

- By gaining a basic understanding of these codes you will always have the ability to see things from a broader perspective, which will enable you to make decisions that are aligned with the highest values of your business or organization. This will be reflective of the desires of the people you serve.

All this will ensure alignment with your highest values so you can reconnect with your passion and live a life of meaning and purpose.

How? I hear you say

You already know the answer. You know the answer the same way you know there's a better way. It's deep down inside. Within.

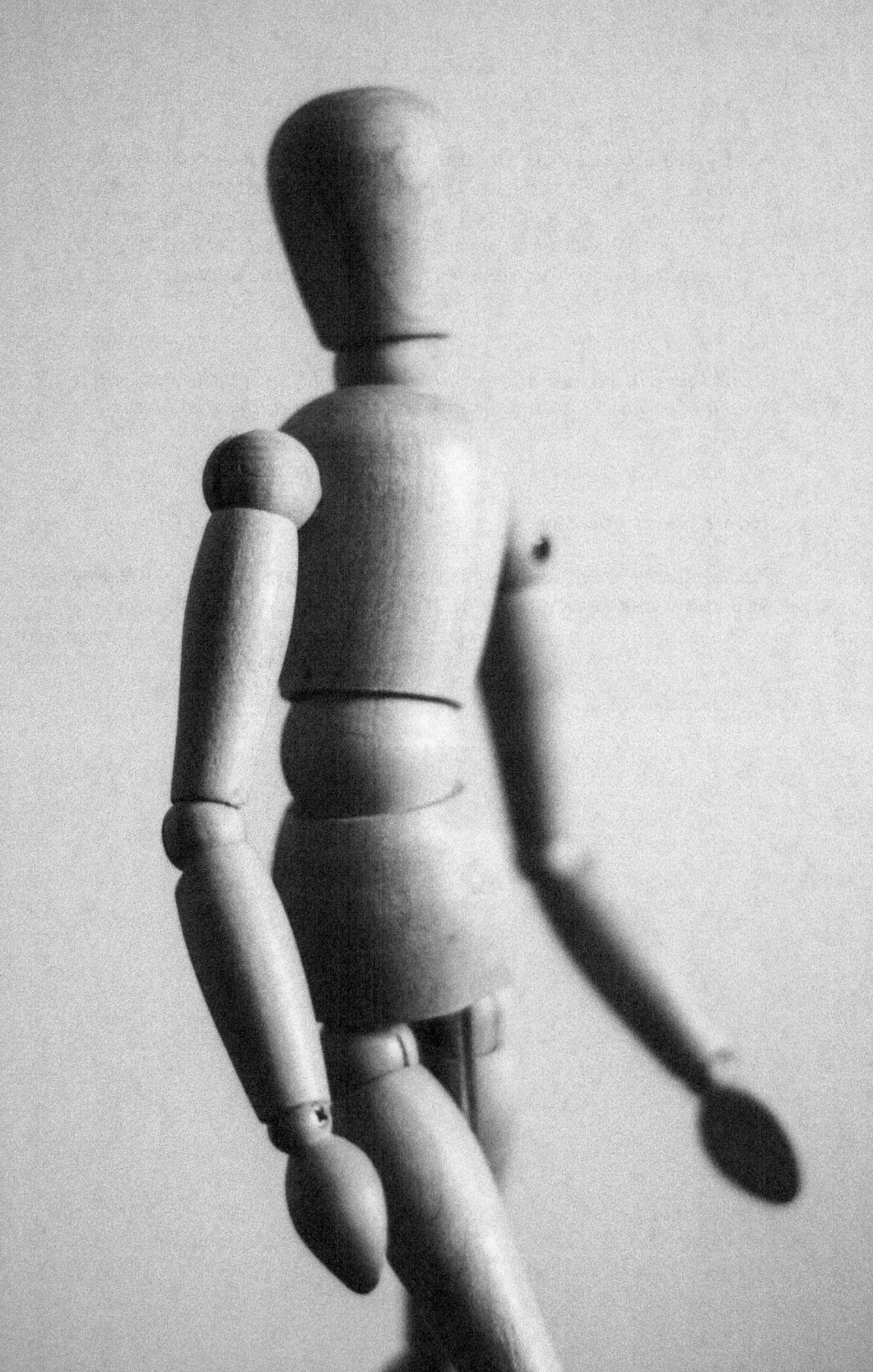

CHAPTER 1

THE ASCENSION LEADERSHIP MODEL

Many years ago, I applied for a job with the Federal Government. It was a strategic role, working on high-level projects and would have required me to move interstate. Working for the Feds had many attractive aspects, and at that point I was ready for a fresh start.

The application process was long and complex. There were myriad questionnaires, psychometric tests, and profiles. One of the strangest parts of the process required me to answer behavioral questions under pressure. The same questions kept coming up, but they were asked in slightly different ways. Of course, the questions were designed to identify behavioral congruency, but they were just so odd. One question I remember was something like, "If you're feeling stressed would you rather break something or hurt small animals?" (Dare I tell them that I'd rather light some incense and meditate?)

These strange questions were intertwined with a deep dive into my personal life and past experiences, stuff from way back. I know it was all designed to provide a comprehensive psychological profile, but none of the options to choose from were reflective of my personal stress management process and it seemed more based upon past actions and historical events than current work style. It didn't seem to account much for the person I was at that time, or even seek to predict how I might have evolved since those past events.

CHAPTER 1: THE ASCENSION LEADERSHIP MODEL

By the end of it I got the sense they were making recruitment decisions based upon who I was ten years ago, I am definitely not the same person I was back then! *Thank Goddess* we have the ability to change our minds and evolve our thinking.

Leadership Profiles

If you're in a leadership role, by now you will have completed several tests, profiles and assessments to identify your personality type, character traits, leadership style even the color of the bus you're driving!

> *Thank Goddess we have the ability to change our minds and evolve our thinking.*

You may have done this testing as a team building or management training exercise, or even as part of your recruitment process. It may have even been the deciding factor for the successful candidate. You've likely seen the Myers Briggs, 6 Sigma, DiSC profile, LSI, GSI, psychographic testing, pattern recognition, lateral thinking...

But no matter how rigorous the testing or expensive the consultant, these profiles are all a construct of someone else's imagination. By design they classify, categorize and pigeonhole you, and there is a margin of error and an inherent flaw because the responses you give will differ from life stage to life stage.

However, once you have been told you are a brown parachute, extravert, dominant, thinker (or whatever combination of buzz words you attached yourself to) you may think that's it and that's all you'll ever be. Typology.

If you have been told you're more of a follower or support crew, you might have just believed it, despite your career history in leadership roles and your aspirations to continue moving up.

Don't get me wrong, these tools can be useful for understanding aspects of ourselves and our potential responses and behavior in a stressful situation. They are, however, still only based on a theoretical model that has been built by the logic of another person and tested in the field in an attempt to be verified as the 'one and only' model to explain human behavior or personality types.

Once you have been codified and classified, you carry that description with you, from role to role. You often reinforce its thinking style and inherent attributes because that's what's expected of you and you solidify your place within that particular pigeonhole, you maybe even struggle to grow much beyond that.

In stark contrast, the **Ascension Leadership Model** increases your flexibility so you can think way outside of the box (or pigeonhole). Using this model, you can adapt to any situation as it assimilates all the typologies and values levels of thinking. It provides a means of transcending the constraints of an established system and resolving challenges by giving you the ability to think and respond like any of the typologies at the time that is most appropriate.

This model shows you how to utilize any mode of perception for problem solving to the benefit of the system within which you are working.

Ascension Leadership leverages domain expertise and left-brain cognitive thinking strategies but is firmly underpinned by intuition and energetic awareness.

Five Pillars

Ascension Leadership is an efficient, synchronistic style that will empower you to move beyond your limitations and activate higher perspectives. The Ascension Leadership Model is based on Five Pillars with each pillar providing a foundation for your cognitive, energetic and intuitive development. Each pillar gives you the ability to step into your creatorship and align with your highest purpose.

While you may achieve some positive results working with one pillar only, by combining these five elements and using each one to support the next, will you open yourself to greater insights and self-mastery.

The model works on the principle of interpromotion among the pillars – each one being necessary to achieve optimal results in the others.

It is an interconnected relationship of growth and promotion that has the flexibility for you to revisit any or all the pillars at a time when you feel it is judicious for you to review and upgrade your perspective.

The 5 Pillars of the Ascension Leadership Model

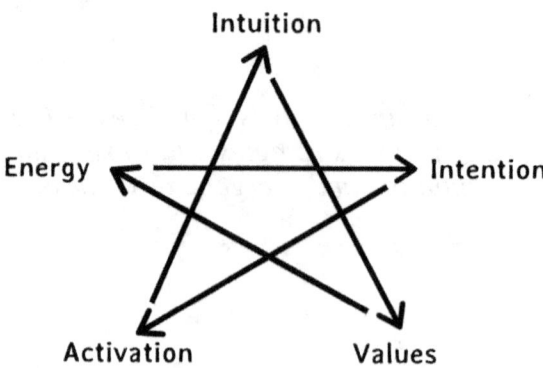

Within the 5 Pillars there are seven key steps which will accelerate your personal growth and ascension. These steps should be taken in order, as they build on the momentum created by the previous step. The steps will be explained in more detail as you progress through this chapter and the book.

Pillar 1 Intuition
Step 1 - Tune in and anchor your personal intuitive process.

Pillar 2 Values
Step 2 - Identify your current values level of thinking.
Step 3 - Resolve outmoded values and evolve your thinking.

Pillar 3 Energy
Step 4 – Liberate the five major emotions from your energy centers.
Step 5 – Raise your energetic vibration.

Pillar 4 Intention
Step 6 - Uncover your purpose and create your future.

Pillar 5 Activation
Step 7 - Activate the fifth dimensional chakras and ascend beyond now.

By working through these Seven Steps and understanding the purpose of each of these pillars, you will identify opportunities to revisit any of the steps in the future.

I recommend reviewing these pillars at times of significant change, to ensure you are energized and clear, or at any time you feel sluggish or want to create more momentum in your life.

CHAPTER 1: THE ASCENSION LEADERSHIP MODEL

The Ascension Leadership Model (ALM) is essentially a model for self-care.

The model can be applied to all areas of life to trigger positive changes and improve personal results. After years of seeing so many women take a fragmented view of how to improve different aspects of their lives, I developed the ALM based on the principle of interpromotion:

1. You will find that the progress you make when applying these steps to leadership and your career will have a positive impact elsewhere.

2. You will notice subtle shifts and changes in your personal life, and you will be inspired to apply these techniques to specific situations and challenges.

3. You will also notice a shift in the way people respond to you and your enhanced energetic vibration.

4. All work you do on yourself, on the inside, is reflected in the world outside of you. It is said that the experiences in our lives are an out-picturing of our internal state. Thus, if you are consistently reviewing and upgrading your internal beliefs, attitudes, energetic vibration and intentions, the world around you will shift into alignment with your new perspectives. As you raise your energetic vibration, you become a magnet which draws a vibrational match – attracting the people, circumstances and opportunities required to support you to achieve your goals.

5. You will also notice your body speaking to you in ways which you may not have been fully aware of in the past. The clarity you gain from working through the Seven Steps will amplify your body's ability to communicate with you on preferred options for improving and maintaining physical wellbeing.

6. You may notice your food cravings and preferences change, such as craving more whole foods, feeling 'off' after eating

certain things such as meat or processed foods, greater sensitivity to stimulants such as sugar, caffeine and alcohol, and a desire for lighter meals.

It is true that the substances you put in your body greatly influence your physical energy and mental clarity. As you work through the steps to tune in to your intuition, your body will tell you how to tune it in even more. And you will notice the cleaner your diet, the clearer your intuition – interconnection.

I make no recommendations for any specific diet to follow and do not advocate extreme, restrictive diets which deprive the body of essential nutrients. I cannot tell you to become a vegan or to stop consuming alcohol or caffeine. Your body will tell you what is best for you. I recommend you try different approaches to eating until you find the one that *feels* right.

For me personally, as I began the process of tuning in and clearing my energy, I stopped eating meat as I noticed it made me feel sluggish and sad. Many years later my body indicated to me a need to reintroduce fish, which I now eat occasionally and feel balanced in doing so.

I certainly notice when I have been through a phase of eating too much heavy food or foods with refined sugars or preservatives, my body gently guides me back to a lighter, whole food regime. I have learnt, over many years of trial, to take note of how my body responds, to make gradual changes, and to be gentle with myself at times when I am diverging from my optimal eating regime.

One of the most supportive things you can do for yourself as you make these changes is ensure you drink plenty of water and get the amount of restful sleep you need to rest your brain and allow your body to heal itself.

Your exercise preferences may also change, perhaps to a desire for lighter more gentle movement such as walking or stretching or increasing cardio as a means of dispersing all the beautiful energy you are resonating with.

I prefer to go walking outdoors, so I can combine mindfulness with gentle exercise and fresh air. I find taking the time to observe the wildlife and have gratitude and appreciation for the trees and lake, the birds and all of nature, gives my body, mind and energy a wonderful boost and deepens my sense of connection.

It is also my time to express my gratitude for my body's vitality and ability to walk in nature and to connect with my physical being.

Again, try different forms of exercise and movement until you find the one that *feels* right. It shouldn't be a task or a chore, instead let it be something you look forward to and enjoy. And there will be times when the best thing you can do for your body is rest. Be okay with that too.

CHAPTER 2

THE LEADER WITHIN – YOUR INTUITIVE SELF

In 2014 I was offered a fantastic opportunity with a local government department. It was a full-time permanent position with a great team. It paid well, had the potential to be creative with a good level of autonomy. The office was only a 20-minute commute, it really ticked all the boxes.

But the more I thought about it, the more anxious I became. I'd start thinking about how good it would be to have a secure job and get back on track, but then I'd notice a feeling in my stomach, a tightness in my throat, a dull ache in my head.

I was becoming increasingly stressed and confused. I needed the security and certainty of a permanent role, but every time I thought about the job, those feelings worsened. I needed to make a decision and let the recruiter know, but I couldn't pick up the phone. I was paralyzed by anxiety. "What's going on?" I yelled on the inside.

"Do not take this job!" was the response from somewhere deep within.

My brain protested based on the data – security, money, career progression….
My body knew what I needed to do.

As soon as I declined the offer, the anxiety lifted. I felt a sense of lightness and serenity that had been unfamiliar to me for some time. The external indicators were telling me it was a bad decision – shocked colleagues, disappointed parents, dwindling bank account. Even though I didn't know what I was going to do next, I felt calm and sure I had made the right decision and was moving towards something bigger. So how could I have that sense of reassurance from my body when my head was so full of logic and reason?

Deliberative Decision-Making versus Intuitive Decision-Making

Deliberative Decision-Making

The science and psychology of decision-making are well documented. Many studies and research projects into deliberative decision-making strategies, and the cognitive processes the brain goes through to arrive at a decision, have demonstrated that our decisions are based on a set of criteria relevant to the situation.

Criteria are logical, left-brain concepts. They are the tangible, measurable, analytical components of thinking which are engaged in planning, forecasting, and rationalizing. The left brain is data-driven, evidence-based, procedural, and often rigid. It is the part of our thinking that needs facts, logic and structure in order to assign meaning and importance and it is heavily context-dependent.

The criteria of decision-making strategies vary from situation to situation. For example, your strategy for deciding to buy a new car is entirely different from your strategy for deciding to buy a new watch or to engage in a joint venture or invest in a new project.

The level of risk versus benefit versus cost is different in each of these scenarios and, depending on your values, the order and importance of your criteria are different from someone else's.

In business, criteria are the fundamental aspects such as cost, value, time, benefit, efficiency, resources, etc. Depending on your industry, it may also include marketability, volume, accessibility, or aesthetics, among many other things.

If we take the example of buying a car, the criteria you need to satisfy to decide on which car might be:

- how much does it cost?
- is it fuel efficient?
- does it look good?

Whereas deciding to partner on a joint venture may have criteria such as:

- does it benefit my business?
- does it add value to my brand or service?
- is there an efficiency gain for output/market reach/resource sharing?

It's also worth noting that your personal values affect your decision-making strategy in terms of how you rank the criteria (are looks more important than cost, for example), as well as any external influences such as stakeholder needs and preferences.

Decisions under pressure

Making decisions when you're under pressure can be more difficult because you perceive the stakes as being higher.

You might be under pressure to decide before a deadline, to decide on the future direction of a project or organization, or to decide on a long-term prospect that will lock things in for a long period and have a knock-on effect on staff and suppliers.

Pressure and stress create unnecessary noise in your head and heighten the nervous system due to the fight or flight response. This response narrows your field of perception, and while it can feel like stress is useful to help you focus, it puts your brain into chaos. Feeling stress or pressure when making a decision is the fastest way to get stuck in a loop and clouded by anxiety and feelings of uncertainty.

Stress is a fight or flight response. It comes from the primitive part of the brain at the back of the head. When the primitive brain is activated, you have access to a very limited range of emotions and behaviors.

Strategies for decision making

Stop and think for a moment — how do you decide? What are the actual processes you go through, the strategy you use, to arrive at a decision? Do you:

a. see something, analyze the data, hear the opinions of others, and then decide?

b. listen to the options, consider the data, and imagine the outcome?

c. read the proposal, get a feel for it, and analyze the benefits?

Cognitive steps

These three basic examples of strategies can be mapped according to the cognitive steps undertaken before arriving at the decision. The basic cognitive processes or inputs are:

- (V) Visual – seeing
- (A) Auditory – hearing
- (K) Kinesthetic – feeling
- (Ad) Auditory Digital – thinking

Let's analyze this based on the same three decision making strategies above and the cognitive steps these strategies use

Decision Making Strategy	Cognitive Steps
a. see something, analyze the data, hear the opinions of others, and then decide?	V + Ad + A = decision
b. listen to the options, consider the data, and imagine the outcome?	A + Ad + V = decision
c. read the proposal, get a feel for it, and analyze the benefits?	V + K + Ad = decision

Your strategy might have three, four, or even five steps depending on the significance of the decision.

Two-step strategies can be risky, for example:

1. see it
2. buy it

This two-step strategy has led to many an ugly outfit in the back of the cupboard, but strategies that have too many steps can be more challenging.

For example:

V + Ad + A + Ad + Ad + A + Ad = decision

The presence of too much Ad – logical, data, analysis – can often lead to second-guessing, self-doubt, decision paralysis and procrastination. It is also time consuming and mentally exhausting.

Exercise

Take some time to map your decision-making strategies. Use three or four examples of decisions of varying importance and review the mental processes you went through before arriving at your final decision.

Take it one step further and make a note of how that decision panned out.

Situation	Process (V, A, K Ad)	= decision (outcome)
e.g. deciding between two candidates for a role on my team	met candidates, heard responses to interview questions, thought about positives and negatives of each, re-read CV, compared experience. V + A + Ad + V + Ad	went with candidate #1 candidate was a good pick, strong skills and X, adds value by X

Another way to decide.

Intuitive Decision-Making

Right-brain decision-making often involves more kinesthetic, or feeling, and is where intuition enters the process.

In business, intuition is often referred to as instincts or gut feelings. Even when making intuitive decisions you draw upon the solid foundation of the skills, knowledge and experience you have in the subject matter – domain expertise, but you are able to connect it all at an unconscious level and gain a physical or 'inner signal' to guide your decision, which is a faster and more energy-efficient process.

This inner signal is your own unique psychophysical process – the brain translating external stimuli (data, options, choices) into a kinesthetic (feeling/emotion).

Everyone's intuitive process is unique

You might get a feeling in your left side when something is positive, but your twin sister may have a sensation in her head when something is positive. This is perhaps one of the reasons there is much consternation about the validity of intuition and its usefulness in business.

Studies into the accuracy of intuitive decision making have been sporadic and at times controversial. However, the emerging interest in intuition and intuitive decision-making in business has resulted in some high-quality studies which have yielded encouraging results.
One study found: *Our behavioral and physiological data, along with evidence-accumulator models, show that non-conscious emotional information can boost accuracy and confidence in a*

concurrent emotion-free decision task, while also speeding up response times.[1]

Further studies into the links between mood and decision making have provided evidence for the theory that — *a sad mood induces people to analyze information carefully, probably fitting well with a deliberative decision strategy and in a happy mood, people tend to act more strongly on their feelings, probably fitting well with an intuitive decision strategy.*[2]

The suggestion here is that intuition is a more natural approach when we are influenced by positive energy and emotions. This is a key reason why the Ascension Leadership Model works through the steps to release negative emotions and activate the energy centers alongside the evolution of the values levels of thinking. The ALM promotes a positive perspective and draws positive people, energy, and experiences to you. Thus, enhancing your natural intuitive style.

The First Pillar of the ALM provides a structured approach to understanding how your intuition 'speaks' to you. This pillar gives you a clear understanding of the signals from your body-mind, and a way to familiarize yourself with that process, so you can cultivate your inner knowing and learn to trust it.

Learning to Trust

How do we know that we know anything?

Patanjali wrote the Yoga Sutras in approximately 200 B.C. The text explores deep existential issues and questions our awareness of consciousness by asking, 'How do we know anything?'

---

1 Lufityanto, Galang, Chris Donkin, and Joel Pearson. "Measuring intuition: nonconscious emotional information boosts decision accuracy and confidence." *Psychological science* 27.5 (2016): 622-634.
2 Marieke de Vries, Rob W. Holland & Cilia L. M. Witteman (2008) Fitting decisions: Mood and intuitive versus deliberative decision strategies, Cognition and Emotion, 22:5, 931-943, DOI: 10.1080/02699930701552580

Patanjali theorized our knowing is based upon four things:

1. its physical appearance
2. the associations you have with it
3. its meaning for you (everything means something different to everyone)
4. its spirit or essence (energy)

Bearing this in mind, ask yourself, how do you know what a chair is? How do you know you are you?

Depending on what you are questioning, your knowing of this can be a simple task or a bit of a mind-bender. Questioning how you know something will always lead you to a greater understanding of the thing you are questioning and a new perspective. But at the very simplest level, you know you know something because it has been taught to you and you trust the source from which you learned it.

If a trusted source like a parent or a teacher tells you 'you are brilliant' your unconscious mind will automatically accept that as truth, just like it will accept a negative suggestion such as 'you are dumb' even if you are keeping up with the other kids in school.

In hypnosis, we call this a 'prestige suggestion'. When a piece of information is offered by a person of authority, the unconscious mind does not question it, instead instantly accepting it as truth and filing it deep within for integration into its world view.

We are subjected to these types of suggestions throughout our lives from parents, teachers, doctors, advertising, celebrities, friends, and social media. But sometimes this information is in direct conflict with what we somehow inherently know.

How many times have you said to yourself, *'I knew that would happen'*?

- Have you ever made a decision or done something and immediately felt 'off'?
- Have you ever just picked up on the 'vibe' of a person or place?
- What about a time you just knew you had to do something or go somewhere or call someone?

Who or what was the source of that knowing?

Call it a hunch, an inkling, a gut feeling, a sense or inner knowing, you most certainly would have had some experiences like this in your life and you likely have a good list of examples you can reflect upon.

> **Exercise**
>
> Take a moment to think about any examples like this in your life and write them down.
>
> Recall each example with as much detail and clarity as you can and then look for the common thread, the feeling, the reason why you knew you knew that thing. What was the key that made you so sure?

Situation	Details	Feeling / Knowing	Action Taken	Why

Now think about the times you did not act and consider why you didn't trust the source.

We don't trust because we've been taught not to. We are told, be logical, rational, use your head, THINK about your decisions.

We have all been in situations where our gut instincts have been questioned, leaving us with feelings of self-doubt. While the adage 'use your head' is quickly giving way to the notion we should lead with our hearts, relearning to trust can be a scary proposition.

Rear Window

There is a classic line in Hitchcock's movie, *Rear Window*. It's about intuition and I must have absorbed it on some level many years ago.

Tom: 'Look, Miss Fremont. That-uh, feminine intuition stuff sells magazines but in real life, it's still a fairy tale. I don't know how many wasted years I've spent tracking down leads based on female intuition.'

Something so small and seemingly insignificant must have permeated my unconscious in some way because for a long time I thought intuition didn't exist or couldn't be trusted.

CHAPTER 2: THE LEADER WITHIN — YOUR INTUITIVE SELF

But luckily for me, when it came time to make some major life changes, my intuition would not be ignored. I began experiencing uncomfortable feelings and recurring hunches that demanded to be explored.

I had been comfortably working in my wellness practice for a few years when the opportunity to work on a strategic plan to manage tourism and destination marketing came along. I was kind of interested and my left brain said, 'Security, reputation, career progression, professional networking.' My Spidey sense was tingling during the second interview, but my left brain decided to accept the offer. The first week in the role I felt awful. Not just nerves, like I kept telling myself, but my body and the world around me flat out yelling at me – chronic headache, the worst UTI I have ever had, unexpected traffic jams, plans falling apart all over the place. 'This is a bad sign, I thought', but I pushed through. It didn't take long for me to discover that the key deliverable of the role had been taken off the table and the leadership of the department was devoid of EQ and people skills.

My intuition was telling me it was a bad decision, but my left brain ignored it. I should have known.

Years before, when I turned down that local government offer in 2014, I had no idea why my guidance was steering me away from the role. Logically it all stacked up, but the feeling I had about it was most definitely 'off.' Turns out, by following my guidance and saying no to that job, the door to an amazing relationship opened. It came from out of nowhere and was in no way expected, but when it showed up, I knew that was the reason why my intuition was guiding me elsewhere. By saying no to something that seemed like a logical choice, I was led to something so profound and special that my life is now forever enriched.

For me, that was the beginning of my gathering of evidence and proof that my intuition could be trusted.

> *The moment you begin to understand that you are the source and that your body is the instrument for gaining the information you need to make a decision, that is the empowering moment you understand that your energy is supportive of your intention to lead a meaningful life.*

Intuitive Exercise

Still not with me? Consider this, do you get a headache every time you think about a task or project? Do you feel nervous, wary, or anxious when you talk to a certain person?

Think about something you are working on right now

- Do you feel light and bright, or flat and low?
- Where in your body do you feel that?
- What aspect of that project makes you feel that way?

Those feelings, the little signals, are your body-mind speaking and they offer valuable clues about possible improvements or changes in direction that will deliver outcomes more aligned with your intentions.

This little exercise is the first step in learning how to recognize and understand the subtle signals your body-mind is giving you. It is the key step in evolving your decision-making into a psychophysical process. A process where your body acts as the mind and quickly accesses everything you need to understand a situation and make a clear distinction between the positive and negative aspects and potential outcomes of any future actions. The more you understand and utilize this inner psychophysical process, the more evidence you will gather to know you can trust it.

CHAPTER 2: THE LEADER WITHIN — YOUR INTUITIVE SELF

ASCENSION LEADERSHIP MODEL STEP 1

Tuning in to your inner process - 'The Inner Resolution Method'

You can cultivate the body's signals and tune into them, so they are always strong and present. The more you check-in and trust these feelings, the better you get at sensing the subtle hints and messages from within.

Exercise

Finding your YES and NO signals from the body

Here is a very simple process to identify when your body is giving you a 'yes' or a positive indication and when it is giving you a 'no' or a negative indication.

Step 1 - Ask yourself a series of questions to which you know the answer is YES

- Notice the feelings, sensations, sounds, or images you are experiencing

- Become aware of how your body is responding to these questions

- Thank your body for giving you these signals and ask to amplify them and make them very clear

- Tell your conscious mind and reaffirm with your body, 'this is my YES'

Step 2 - Ask yourself a series of questions to which you know the answer is definitely NO.

- Bring your awareness to the feelings, sensations, sounds or images you are experiencing and notice how they differ to the feelings and sensations of your yes questions

- Thank your body for giving you these signals and ask to amplify them and make them very clear

- Tell your conscious mind and reaffirm with your body, 'this is my NO'

Step 3 – Note your psychophysical process

	EMOTION or SENSATION e.g. tingling, heat, vibration	LOCATION IN BODY	COLOURS OR SOUNDS
YES SIGNAL			
NO SIGNAL			

Step 4 - Ask yourself a series of questions related to everyday activities and scenarios, e.g. diet, recreational activities, etc.

- Notice the response and your level of conscious agreement with the answer
- Is the response your body is giving you different to what your conscious mind thinks or wants?

Step 5 - Use this technique as much as possible to strengthen and familiarize it

- Make notes of your outcomes to gather evidence to reinforce that it is safe to trust your intuition

As you are gathering your evidence, understand that the quality of your questions is very important. For example, if you ask your body 'is this good?' your inner knowing has no real context and will not be able to give you a clear response. Your questions should be clear and specific to provide the information you need to make an informed decision. Here are a few examples of clear questions to which you can gain a 'yes' or 'no' or positive or negative response.

- Is this the best option for me right now?
- Does this food cause inflammation in my body?
- Is this action for my highest good?
- Do I need more information before making a final decision?
- Is it best for me to wait until tomorrow/next week before acting?
- Is my body dehydrated right now?

- Is there an alternative option which is better than this one?
- Can I trust this person concerning this situation?

By using this technique in everyday life, you are telling your unconscious, inner process and intuition that you are willing to listen. The more you use it, the stronger it will get and soon you will be feeling those familiar feelings of positive and negative without having to ask questions.

> *Your intuition is there to give you clues and directions on the best possible actions to take in any area of life and, as you begin to trust the small things, you will begin to know you can tune in and ask for help on the big stuff – career and business decisions, financial matters, key relationships.*

The key is to follow the guidance and trust it. You may receive a response that you are not happy with. For example, you might ask "Is this chocolate cookie for my optimal health?", receive a 'no', but choose to eat it anyway.

In that instance you can say to your inner self, "Thank you for the information, I am going to go ahead and eat it and I am willing to be 100% responsible for any consequences (headache, sugar jitters)." In that way, you are reassuring your intuition that you are not ignoring it and so it will be happy to stick around and continue to guide you.

Let your intuition know you are willing to listen to and trust its messages and that you will take positive action to align you to your purpose. Your intuition is there to give you clues and directions on the best possible actions to take in any area of life and, as you begin to trust the small things, you will begin to know you can tune in and ask for help on the big stuff – career and business decisions, financial matters, key relationships.

Because you have a background of experience and subject matter knowledge to draw upon, trusting your intuition when making business decisions is not just blind faith or throwing caution to the wind.

This domain expertise is the foundation for understanding a situation but going through the process of analyzing every single bit of data is time-consuming and inefficient. Your intuition coalesces this knowledge at an unconscious level in a matter of moments to provide physical signals that are consciously understood and context-appropriate.

You have now discovered the Inner Resolution Method. This is a way to consistently make informed, guided decisions without stress, overthinking, and second-guessing. The primitive brain no longer rules you.

If you'd like support in working through the Inner Resolution Method, contact me directly at hello@theleader-within.com

---

Psychic Vs Intuitive — Is it just semantics?

Intuition is defined as:

a. the ability to understand something instinctively, without the need for conscious reasoning

b. something that one knows or considers likely from instinctive feeling rather than conscious reasoning

And if you look up psychic in the dictionary you will find:

a. relating to or denoting faculties or phenomena that are apparently inexplicable by natural laws, especially involving telepathy or clairvoyance

b. relating to the soul or mind

In the context of someone being psychic, you have probably heard of the terms Clairvoyance, Clairaudience, Clairsentience, Claircognizance and Clairgustience.

These are our metaphysical or intuitive senses, the ways in which we perceive inner information. So, whether we care to acknowledge it or not, our psychophysical process must draw upon information and insights coming to us through one or more of these 'psychic' senses.

Consciously observing your psychophysical process will enhance your awareness of these senses and give you more ways to quickly understand and read a situation. The more ways you have of knowing, the more confirmation you have upon which to build trust and confidence.

Even Oprah Winfrey says, "Learning to trust your instincts, using your intuitive sense of what's best for you, is paramount for any lasting success."

So, you've got valid scientific studies and research into intuition, and Oprah sharing tips and techniques on how to tune in, what else do you need to go within?

CHAPTER 3

WHERE ARE YOU NOW - A BASELINE FOR THE ASCENDING LEADER

Of all the personality profile models, assessments, tests, and sectors I've come across, I've never felt comfortable with any of the results or the way in which they defined me. I've even tried to 'fuck the system' by answering the questions in the opposite or most moderate way possible and have still been presented with a congenial and somewhat incongruent explanation of who I am and my leadership style.

Surely there is a more organic way of understanding personal attributes and potential behaviors that flexes and grows with the person themselves?

Let's go to New York
Clare W Graves (Ph.D. Psychology) was a professor at Union College in Schenectady, New York.

He taught models of psychology, behaviorism and humanistics. One day his graduating students asked him, of all the models he had just taught them, which was the correct one?

Graves had no answer to this. Each was a theoretical model that could be supported through field testing and each had its limitations and contradictions. But no one model was evidently better or more correct than the other. The question still lingered, so Graves asked his students.

This sparked a long-term data collection phase which would eventually uncover thematic existential issues humans face as they progress through life. These levels of existence had not previously been identified or examined in any major work explaining humanity but were naturally occurring, recurrent and clear across the significant data collected by Graves and his peers over time.

Graves collated these thematic issues from all over the world and grouped them into levels. The levels he discovered explain *how* a person thinks based on their values or world view and demonstrate the possibility and likelihood of transition and evolution in thinking, whereas all the popularly accepted frameworks of the time focused on *what* they think and kept them in the box of their personality type diagnosis.

Graves continued to collect and collate data to support his Existence Theory and the data continued to confirm what he had initially discovered.

Existence Theory
This theory makes sense to me because I see a strong correlation with the energetic aspects, or themes, of our chakras and the life-stage challenges associated with those chakras. The **Graves Values model** demonstrates a progression of ideas and concepts as it takes us from a singular survival focus along a spectrum to a place of connectedness and desire for making a global contribution.

As we evolve ideas and the ability to grasp new concepts, we increase our ability to adapt to change and step more fully into ourselves, aligning with our sense of purpose. We begin to see where there are obstacles that are stopping us from moving forward or achieving the next level of thought or consciousness. Each transition point, major crisis or challenge – political, environmental, social or personal, causes us to think beyond our current level and evolve to the next, where greater potential and flexibility exists.

As a leader in a decision making role or a position of influence, your values play strongly into your ability to adapt to change, your ambition, your interpersonal style, your level of risk aversion, your motivation to build, grow, expand, your desire to serve and your willingness to comply.

Our goal is to understand the essence of each of the Values Levels so you can identify any obstacles and evolve to the next level of thinking for your ultimate benefit and that of your business and your community.

Understanding the Graves Values Levels

The conscious mind needs structure to fully grasp and understand a concept, so Graves described his *Emergent Cyclical Levels of Existence Theory (or ECLET)* as a double helix spiral of levels to demonstrate that all humans evolve not just physically, but also socially and psychologically in a lifetime.

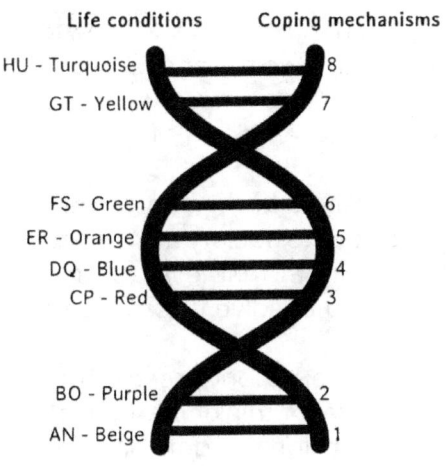

Referred to as Values Levels, each stage of conscious awareness and actualization is assigned a number, a color, and an alpha code. The numbers are simply a way to notate the levels of the spiral and the alpha code is used to represent the life conditions and coping mechanisms. The first number correlates with the level in the spiral e.g. 1 = A, 2 = B, 3 = C, etc. and the second number represents the default coping mechanism or thinking style.

The colors are not symbolic in any way and do not relate to the chakras. They are merely another way of notating that Values Level or world view, e.g. a blue way of thinking.

It is important to understand that no one level is better or worse than another and each level has its own positive and negative aspects, challenges, and opportunities. Every person can reach an understanding of each level and, once you have experienced and resolved a level and moved beyond it, you are able to draw from the perspective of each of the levels you have transcended.

It is important to understand that no one level is better or worse than another and each level has its own positive and negative aspects, challenges, and opportunities.

Values Levels are essentially the world view or context through which a person views the world, and Graves's Existence Theory identifies what people unconsciously seek out in life at each psychological level of existence.

You are born into a Values Level due to the traditions, culture, beliefs and structures of the society and environment around you and you will only operate at that level for as long as that way of thinking can support you to solve the challenges you face.

Once the views of that level no longer serve you, you are compelled to think beyond that level of thinking and evolve to the next. This can explain why you just don't understand or connect with some people, or why some people view you in a totally inaccurate way. Understanding each level provides the opportunity to identify the challenges a person, group or whole of society will face. It also gives clues on the most effective and relevant ways to solve problems that will empower that person or group and allow them to evolve to the next natural level without force or resistance. In his 1974 article, *Human Nature Prepares for a Momentous Leap* (The Futurist) Clare Graves described each of the levels as per the tables below.

You will see that I have also included my ***Ascension Leadership Model Interpretation (ALM Interpretation)***, to provide a context for how you might see these Values Levels expressed today.

Level / Code / Color: 1 A-N BEIGE	
Learning System:	Habituation
Thinking Style:	Automatic
Motivational System:	Physiological
Specific Motivation:	Periodic physiological needs
Means Values:	No conscious value system
Ends Values:	No conscious value system
Nature of Existence:	Automatic
Memes:	Survival, biogenic needs satisfaction, reproduction, satisfy instinctive urge.
Challenges:	Reactive, biologically driven, living in a state of nature, limited sense of cause and effect; there is very little of this level remaining, although people can regress into it (e.g. Alzheimer's).
Problems of Existence:	Maintaining physiological stability

ALM Interpretation:

You are not likely to see VL1 behavior at your workplace or in today's society in general. VL1 behaviors support existence at the very basic level, it is purely about survival however, a person or group may revert to this behavioral style in life-threatening illness or significant destabilization such as homelessness, war or natural disaster.

CHAPTER 3: WHERE ARE YOU NOW – A BASELINE FOR THE ASCENDING LEADER

Level / Code / Color: 2 B-O PURPLE	
Learning System:	Classical conditioning
Thinking Style:	Autistic
Motivational System:	Assurance
Specific Motivation:	Aperiodic physiological needs
Means Values:	Traditionalism
Ends Values:	Safety
Nature of Existence:	Tribalistic
Memes: Animistic:	Placate spirit realm, honor ancestors, protection from harm, family bonds.
Challenges:	Subsumed in the group, no separate identity of 'I' – the focus is on co-operation, sharing, ritual; conflict will endanger the tribe, who have the forces of nature to contend with.
Problems of Existence:	Achievement of relative safety.

ALM Interpretation:

VL2 best describes tribal or clan situations. A small group following a 'Chief' and honoring traditions and superstitions. Strong beliefs in the supernatural, rituals, talismans. Structured roles based upon kinship, seniority, elders. Actions are for the highest good of the group.

Basic military training is based on this principle – a powerful authority (drill sergeant) passing on survival skills, teaching routines, breaking a soldier down, and meting out operant conditioning. You may see this behavioral style in your workplace if you are working in a military capacity or within traditional cultural frameworks.

Level / Code / Color: 3 C-P RED	
Learning System:	Operant conditioning
Thinking Style:	Egocentric
Motivational System:	Survival
Specific Motivation:	Psychological survival
Means Values:	Exploitation
Ends Values:	Power
Nature of Existence:	Egocentric
Memes:	Power/action, asserting self to dominate others, control, sensory pleasure.
Challenges:	Breaking away from the tribe, impulsive, seeking respect, honor and avoiding shame and establishing the self, might is right; the world is adversarial, uncaring, only raw power will let me prevail.
Problems of Existence:	Living with self-awareness.

ALM Interpretation:

These are the tough guys – the rebels, gang leaders and bullies. They are rule breakers and thrill-seekers, lacking impulse control or long-term plans. Often found at the lower-social economic end of society and working in high-risk, hard labor roles, or menial or transient work. There is a strong association with hierarchy, the 'top dog' calls the shots. Apparent in organized crime rings such as the Mafia, this is empire building and ruling all. VL3 can also produce heroes and 'Lone-Ranger' defenders of society. Think comic book superheroes.

CHAPTER 3: WHERE ARE YOU NOW – A BASELINE FOR THE ASCENDING LEADER

Level / Code / Color: 4 D-Q BLUE	
Learning System:	Avoidant learning
Thinking Style:	Absolutistic
Motivational System:	Security
Specific Motivation:	Order, meaning
Means Values:	Sacrifice
Ends Values:	Salvation
Nature of Existence:	Saintly
Memes:	Absolutistic: stability/order, obedience to earn reward later, meaning, purpose, certainty.
Challenges:	Emerges from the chaos of C-P – obedience to rightful authority, binary thinking, categorizing, deny self for 'the one right way', stability and security is achieved through sacrifice and submission, doing things by the book/manual; bringing in new norms undermines control/authority.
Problems of Existence:	Achieving ever-lasting peace of mind.

ALM Interpretation:

Anything structured, and system driven; law and rules, the police force, military, government structures, unions, communism, religious organizations. This is 'by the book' compliance, fulfilling of duties and obligations. Stability and long-term planning are key factors, superannuation/retirement plans, work hard now for a promotion later. If it has an organizational chart it is VL4!

Level / Code / Color: 5 E-R ORANGE	
Learning System:	Expectancy
Thinking Style:	Multiplistic
Motivational System:	Independence
Specific Motivation:	Adequacy, competency
Means Values:	Scientism
Ends Values:	Materialism
Nature of Existence:	Materialistic
Memes:	Opportunity/success, competing to achieve results, influence, autonomy.
Challenges:	Emerges from the rigidity of D-Q, how to maneuver rather than comply, many ways and criteria rather than one right way or set of standards, goal directed, independent, self-sufficient, confident, experiment to find the best among many possible choices, future oriented and competitive; work for the good life and abundance, the winners deserve their rewards.
Problems of Existence:	Conquering the physical universe.

ALM Interpretation:

VL5 is breaking out of the system and going it alone. Small business, entrepreneurs, personal goals to improve own lifestyle. This VL brings in the concepts of abundance and material gain which, if unchecked, can become the pursuit of goals at the expense of others or negative impacts on society, environment, etc. Most of our economic activity and ideas around trade and consumerism is VL5. It is capitalism, mass-consumerism, super-yachts, mansions, and plastic surgery.

CHAPTER 3: WHERE ARE YOU NOW – A BASELINE FOR THE ASCENDING LEADER

Level / Code / Color: 6 F-S GREEN	
Learning System:	Observational
Thinking Style:	Relativistic
Motivational System:	Affiliation
Specific Motivation:	Love, affiliation
Means Values:	Sociocentric
Ends Values:	Community
Nature of Existence:	Personalistic
Memes: Relativistic:	Harmony/love, joining for mutual growth, awareness, belonging.
Challenges:	Emerges in response to the excesses of E-R, can't do it on my own and need to collaborate with others, group membership highly valued, tolerates ambiguity through encountering diverse perspectives, requires trust, doesn't want to hurt others; high empathy and sensitivity to others – everybody counts.
Problems of Existence:	Living with the Human element.

ALM Interpretation:

Group movements to improve circumstances for all – environmentalism, women's rights, P.E.T.A, support groups. This is the peace and love mindset. Feelings, group consensus and harmony are key drivers. Flatter organization structures than VL4 these organizations focus on group activities and a team approach to problem-solving. VL6 easily expresses emotions – hugging, group hugs and are the carers or 'momma bears' in a group. Your VL6 colleagues will be totally on board with workplace meditation or mindfulness activities!

Level / Code / Color: 7 G-T YELLOW	
Learning System:	All learning systems open
Thinking Style:	Systemic
Motivational System:	Existential
Specific Motivation:	Self-worth
Means Values:	Accepting
Ends Values:	Existence
Nature of Existence:	Cognitive
Memes:	Systemic: independence/self-worth, fitting a living system, knowing good questions.
Challenges:	Demands flexibility, autonomy, accepts paradoxes and uncertainties, self-interest without harm to others, curiosity, learns from a variety of sources, contextual thinkers, can see things but not always be able to explain them, great awareness of what they do and don't understand, punished by conventional education and corporate structures; not motivated by fear of survival, God or social approval, guilt and reward motivators don't work – seeks to do well without compulsive drives and ambitiousness.
Problems of Existence:	Restoring viability to a disordered world.

ALM Interpretation:

VL7 is like the second iteration of VL1 – it is survival driven, but of the mental and spiritual nature as opposed to the physical of VL1. There is a high level of self-awareness and self-acceptance and a strong understanding of how and when to act appropriately in a situation – it is context-driven. VL7s like diversity and variety but dislike anything unnecessary such as long meetings with no agenda and pointless phone calls!

CHAPTER 3: WHERE ARE YOU NOW – A BASELINE FOR THE ASCENDING LEADER

Level / Code / Color: 8 H-U TURQUOISE	
Learning System:	All learning systems open
Thinking Style:	Differential
Motivational System:	Experience
Specific Motivation:	Unknown
Means Values:	Experiencing
Ends Values:	Communion
Nature of Existence:	Experientialistic
Theorized meme:	Global community / life force, survival of life on a fragile Earth, consciousness.
Problem of Existence:	What this level will create still not fully known; may be holistic focus on the wellbeing of all entities, comfortable with many paths to knowing; self is part of a larger non-localized field. Accepting existential dichotomies.

ALM Interpretation:

This is like the second iteration of VL2, but with a metaphysical focus. VL8 sees the dysfunction of the other levels and works on the internal to resolve external conditions. This may often be interpreted by other VLs as apathy or being 'off with the 'fairies.' VL8 is highly flexible and easily able to connect with any resource or thinking/ behavioral style of other VLs to achieve desired outcomes.

Where are you now?

In order to evolve your thinking, we need to first get an understanding of your current Values Level, which is kind of like your set point for thinking. We want to fully understand where you are now, so you can resolve any limitations you might be experiencing and move to the next level. This would give you an even greater potential for meaningful communication and problem-solving.

Whatever level you are at, you will have the flexibility to draw from the concepts and insights from that level and any level that has come before that. The further along the spiral you are, the more flexibility you have.

Identify Your Leadership Vales

Exercise

ASCENSION LEADERSHIP MODEL STEP 2 – Values Level Assessment

To discover where you are now, respond to the concepts below in the way that most describes you or reflects what is important to you with either 'strongly agree', 'strongly disagree' or 'don't care.'

'Don't care' doesn't mean you are apathetic or unsympathetic, it just means there is no emotional charge connected to that concept, you are neutral. Respond to these concepts in the context of leadership.

CHAPTER 3: WHERE ARE YOU NOW – A BASELINE FOR THE ASCENDING LEADER

STRONGLY AGREE	DON'T CARE	STRONGLY DISAGREE	CONCEPT
Part 1 Each answer of STRONGLY AGREE and STRONGLY DISAGREE is worth 2 points. DON'T CARE is worth 0			
			It is important for me to maintain certain rituals
			Old superstitions are based on truth
			I talk to my car
			I carry lucky charms
			Safety in numbers
			TOTAL
Part 2 Each answer of STRONGLY AGREE and STRONGLY DISAGREE is worth 1 point. DON'T CARE is worth 0			
			Survival of the fittest
			I make my own rules
			Win or go down in a blaze of glory
			I'm here for a good time not a long time
			I crave adventure and excitement
			TOTAL

STRONGLY AGREE	DON'T CARE	STRONGLY DISAGREE	CONCEPT
Part 3 Each answer of STRONGLY AGREE and STRONGLY DISAGREE is worth 1 point. DON'T CARE is worth 0			
			I follow the rules and respect all authority
			My life is about discipline and self-discipline
			Stability is important
			A place for everything and everything in its place
			We all should be contributing to society
			TOTAL
Part 4 Each answer of STRONGLY AGREE and STRONGLY DISAGREE is worth 1 point. DON'T CARE is worth 0			
			I am very focused on personal achievement
			It is very important to be logical
			I want to be an expert
			I am a leader
			I'm all for calculated risks
			TOTAL

CHAPTER 3: WHERE ARE YOU NOW – A BASELINE FOR THE ASCENDING LEADER

STRONGLY AGREE	DON'T CARE	STRONGLY DISAGREE	CONCEPT
Part 5 Each answer of STRONGLY AGREE and STRONGLY DISAGREE is worth 1 point. DON'T CARE is worth 0			
			All you need is love
			I feel harmonious with myself and others
			Consensus is important – every voice should be heard
			I always look for the good in others
			Inner peace is achieved by pleasing others
			TOTAL
Part 6 Each answer of STRONGLY AGREE and STRONGLY DISAGREE is worth 2 points. DON'T CARE is worth 0			
			I know myself and my strengths
			Change can be difficult
			There are always many solutions to a problem
			I like to be in control of my projects
			People who care about people make better leaders
			TOTAL

How to interpret the answers.

Enter your totals in the table below

PART	STRONGLY AGREE TOTAL	STRONGLY DISAGREE TOTAL	VALUES LEVEL
PART 1			VL2 – Clan
PART 2			VL3 – Self Rule
PART 3			VL4 – System
PART 4			VL5 - Entrepreneur
PART 5			VL6 – Group Causes
PART 6			VL7 - Independent

Scoring

The highest STRONGLY AGREE totals in a part indicate your current Values Level. If you have two totals that are very close, it suggests you are currently shifting and evolving into the next level. It's not uncommon to have high scores in two levels and possibly even a third which indicates an ongoing resolution of the lower level.

High totals in the STRONGLY DISAGREE column indicate a high level of rejection of that Values Level, which reflects unresolved issues around the key themes or ideas of that level. Resolving those highly rejected levels is where you will make rapid progress in your leadership ascension and set yourself up to move fully into or beyond your current level of thinking.

You can download a more comprehensive analysis of your Values Level at www.theleader-within.com

CHAPTER 3: WHERE ARE YOU NOW – A BASELINE FOR THE ASCENDING LEADER

Frequently in our professional lives, we work on projects or in organizations where the values of the 'company' are not totally aligned with our own values. And we often see examples of organizational values that do not align with the values of their end-users or communities they serve. It is possible to identify the Values Level of an organization or leadership group and, where necessary, align the values of individuals to increase the cohesiveness of the leadership group and productivity of the organization.

For more information on corporate values alignment visit www.theleader-within.com

By working through the **Ascension Leadership Model**, you will be able to resolve highly rejected levels and evolve your thinking so you can access all thinking systems and find new ways to transcend organizational challenges for your core business.

This approach to leadership and organizational development has never been more relevant and more important. A major paradigm shift is coming, a shift in thinking and a restructuring of outdated systems and traditional ways of doing business. There is increasing pressure on business and government to be more transparent and equitable.

Global economics can no longer be driven by unsustainable practices, short-term visions, and unbalanced power structures. Private interests and hidden agendas by design, disempower the majority and elevate only a very few. It is now time to evolve beyond the 'me first' mentality. We must lead from a place of compassion and understanding that everyone has a valuable contribution to make and is deserving of opportunity and equitable outcomes.

The Dalai Lama said, "The world will be saved by the Western woman." The keyword there is woman.

I believe that women will be at the forefront of the shift

Personally, many of us feel a call to better serve our communities and make a greater contribution. This calling is not so we can feel important, or become rich celebrities, or grow our social media following. It is a result of an inner yearning to create meaning in our lives and fulfill our highest purpose.

My contribution to this evolution is the sharing of the **Ascension Leadership Model** so that more women will have the awareness and knowledge to transcend perceived limitations and fully embrace their personal power and ability to create positive, purposeful outcomes for themselves, their families and their communities.

CHAPTER 4

LIBERATE THE LEADER WITHIN

Everything is connected and nothing operates in isolation.

Working in one life area will have a ripple effect on all life areas, and consciously working in all life areas will supercharge every aspect of your experience.

This is important to remember because, while we are looking at your values in the context of your leadership or work and career, you will notice that any positive steps forward in that area will have positive impacts everywhere else.

Your values will vary from context to context and you may place certain behaviors or habits as being of higher importance from one area to the next, but each is connected and will have a flow-on effect to the other. As you evolve your thinking around the way you work, you will notice shifts in attitudes around the way you live, your health and personal care, your spirituality and even your relationships.

This chapter will reveal to you any lingering issues that need resolving in any of the Values Levels so you can move along the spiral and increase your flexibility.

Resolving and moving beyond a Values Level doesn't mean that Values Level is done and finished and never to be revisited again. What it does is give you the ability to draw from that level, and any level before it, and call upon those strengths and aspects when a situation calls for it. The further along the spiral you are, the more Values Levels you can integrate, and the greater your flexibility and self-sufficiency.

ASCENSION LEADERSHIP MODEL STEP 3

Resolution of a Values Level is about letting go of outmoded attitudes, limiting beliefs, and unresourceful behaviors and reactions to life circumstances. It is also about moving beyond the existential problems connected to each level and seeing life from a broader perspective.

As you move through and subsequently resolve a Values Level, you will open up the thinking systems associated with that level which will allow you to understand the motivations of those operating within that level and their key existential needs and motivations. You will clearly see others and understand their world views and the challenges they face.

The strategies are based upon what you need to let go of and the energy you need to step into, to transition to the next level.

In this chapter, I have suggested a key strategy to resolve each of the Values Levels. The strategies are based upon what you need to let go of and the energy you need to step into, to transition to the next level. Where you have a high rejection of a Values Level, follow the process to resolve that level, and if you need to resolve more than one level, I strongly recommend you wait at least a month between each resolution to allow for the shift to fully integrate. During this time you will have the opportunity to review what you are letting go of, to understand why you held it for so long, and to identify new awarenesses that have enabled you to move beyond the limitations associated with that level.

This also gives you the time to honor the space between what was and where you are going. Have gratitude for and fully accept every part of your past. All your life experiences are important and have made a valuable contribution to who you are today. It also helps you to realize it is time to let go and transition to the next level.

Remember, you can't skip any of the levels and you really need to have an understanding and experience of each level to move to the next. All growth happens as it should, at the time that is most right for you.

> All growth happens as it should, at the time that is most right for you.

The following resolution strategies can be done as a visualization or meditation, or a letter written to yourself telling the story of your transition. Where you have personal experiences or memories of past events connected to the themes in the strategies, use them as the basis for the process. As we are working in the context of your leadership, draw upon any work or career-related experiences for the resolution process. This will ensure any limiting perceptions about your ability or worthiness as a leader are dissolved and your career ambitions are aligned to a higher level of consciousness.

There are also some positive actions to take which will allow the changes to integrate on all levels of your Being:

- spiritually
- mentally

- physically and
- emotionally

Write down the shifts

I highly recommend writing down any shifts (energetic, emotional, behavioral) you notice over the month after each level is complete. The transition itself is a significant experience and the journaling process will deepen your experience as old attitudes emerge before release. It will also give you an opportunity to reflect on past events and find new meanings for them. This awareness will be very helpful when it comes to releasing blockages in the energy body that are connected to certain chakras and life stages (Step 4).

When working through a resolution strategy, it's important you take the time and space for this process:

- Find a time when you will be uninterrupted and can work through the strategy at your own pace.
- Make yourself comfortable and begin by bringing awareness to your breath, comfortably deepening your breath and relaxing your body.
- Imagine all tension and worry leaving your body on the out-breath and breathe in loving healing energy.
- Allow yourself the time to connect with the memories and emotions that come up during the process and be gentle with yourself as you heal and release these connections.

Resolution Strategies

VL2 – Resolve feelings of being a victim and gain understanding and self-awareness.

Step 1:
Go back to a time in your life where you have felt defenseless or a sense of abandonment. If there has been more than one occasion, go back to the very first time. Go back into that moment and see the events through your own eyes. Notice the situation and any other people.

Step 2:
Bring in a feeling of realization and knowing that you deserve to speak up and recall the many things that you are capable of doing on your own. Decide now that you *are* capable and independent. Recognize that the other people connected to this event are acting out of their own best interests and there is no intent to harm you in any way.

Step 3:
Now imagine floating up out of your body and watch yourself standing strong in your power as you thank these people. Notice that any energetic cords of attachment between you dissolve. See yourself standing strong and confidently, surrounded in a glowing ball of pure white light. Feel an activation in your solar plexus (lower chest) and heart chakra and notice a feeling of lightness and clarity.

Step 4:

Positive actions to anchor the resolution

- Schedule an activity to do for yourself and by yourself, such as go to the movies or take yourself out for dinner.

- Take a short break alone or with someone outside of your family or regular friendship group.
- Wear a different outfit, one that is a more daring style for you and unlike the current trend or mainstream style.

VL3 – Resolve feelings of hurt and rejection and gain self-acceptance

Step 1:
Bring full awareness to your body and recognize any feelings of guilt, shame, or rage that you carry. Acknowledge these as a normal part of the human experience and recognize that you are now able to let them go as you decide to have more certainty in your life. Notice any shifts in your body as the guilt, shame and rage are totally dissolved. Feel your body realigning as your internal signals for 'yes' and 'no' become stronger and clearer.

Step 2:
Visualize yourself tuning in to your body and asking questions about positive actions. See yourself taking guided action and fully accepting who you are and your unique qualities. Feel a warmth expanding in your sacral chakra (lower stomach) as your mind, body and spirit reconnects and fully integrates expanded thinking styles.

Positive actions to anchor the resolution

- Continue to tune in and use your body's 'yes' and 'no' signals, use them daily in a broad range of situations.
- Join a group with similar interests, such as a book club or spiritual development group. Ensure that within this group you actively participate in conversations and activities.
- Repeat this affirmation daily to yourself in the mirror, 'I love and accept myself'.

VL4 – Let go of unfulfilled expectations and go with the flow

Step 1:
Go back to a time in your life where you may have felt guilt and acknowledge you were doing the best you could with the information you had. Release the guilt and notice if the actions were motivated by a feeling of being undeserving or a feeling of unworthiness. Allow any feelings of disappointment in yourself or others to totally dissolve.

Step 2:
Imagine a scenario where you decide that you are done with having slightly less than enough or barely enough. Feel a sense of excitement enter your body as you realign to a feeling of total worthiness. Recognize a deep inner knowing that you deserve an abundance of all things.

Step 3:
Visualize any feelings of guilt or self-righteousness completely dissolve and disappear. Acknowledge and commit to being more assertive with authority, speaking up and voicing your opinion and feel an activation of energy in your throat.

Positive actions to anchor the resolution

- Brag about yourself or your accomplishments to a friend or family member.
- Ask your boss for a salary review or additional resources.
- Buy something or have an experience specifically to indulge and spoil yourself.

VL5 – Let go of control and find peace, faith and trust

Step 1:
Make a list of your fears. Ask yourself why you fear these things or experiences. Is there any evidence as to why these are a threat to you?

Step 2:
Thank your unconscious mind for protecting you and ask it to release any feelings of fear or not being enough. Ask your unconscious mind to come up with three new ways to protect you and increase your confidence and self-worth.

Step 3:
Visualize a ball of light at the base of your spine and see it grow and intensify. As it gets bigger visualize all fear completely leaving your body. Feel an activation in your heart chakra as a deep sense of inner peace and knowing settles in your body.

Positive actions to anchor the resolution

- Join a volunteer group and work in a role that will not receive any public acknowledgment.
- Practice regular meditation and self-reflection.
- Talk about your feelings with someone you don't know well.

VL6 – Surrender roles and duties and gain commitment

Step 1:
Go back to a time in your life where you felt sad, lonely or powerless. If there is more than one occasion, go back to the very first time. Notice if you have played out any patterns of excluding yourself or staying on the edges. Recognize any barriers you have created to keep others at a distance.

Step 2:
Visualize yourself moving from the edges into the center of a group or crowd, see any barriers disappear as you move closer to the center of the group. Notice a feeling of comfort and warmth in your heart chakra as you are surrounded by the group and decide now to be a part of a shared idea or plan that has positive outcomes for many people.

Positive actions to anchor the resolution

- Set yourself a task to achieve with a deadline. Make it a significant task, something that is meaningful to you and your goals and will take some work to achieve. Complete the task within the set time frame.

- Identify two or three new habits or behaviors you would like to introduce into your life to create positive changes. Decide how and when you will implement these, e.g. frequency, intensity, duration. Begin. Track the behavior for the first few weeks until it becomes a lasting change.

- Undertake independent learning of a new topic or skill. Do this through an on-line course or teach yourself with the aid of videos and books.

VL7 – Let go of social expectations, speak out and be a conscious leader

Step 1:
Go back to a time where you felt misunderstood or as though everyone else was on a different wavelength. Consider the different life experiences of those other people and recognize that everyone evolves at a different pace.

Step 2:
Make a decision now to find others at your level to work and collaborate with and acknowledge your capacity to assist others to get on their path. Feel that decision as a tingling in your forehead and at the top of your head as it integrates into your entire body.

Positive actions to anchor the resolution

- Find an opportunity to explain your ideas to a large group of people and be patient with anyone who does not fully understand.

- Write a compassionate letter to someone who has misunderstood you or who is not as strong. Have a sympathetic discussion and acknowledge where they are in their journey. Thank them for what they have taught you. You don't need to send this letter.

Working through the strategy for each of the Values Levels in which you scored a high number of strongly disagrees, will clear away any connection to old attitudes that are stopping you from moving forward.

It's important to do this because the more connection to stagnant energy you have, the harder it is to find clarity, be decisive, have meaningful supportive relationships, or work towards your purpose.

Meaning and purpose

Finding meaning and purpose in life is not difficult when you are aligned with your highest values. There's a lot of talk these days and self-help books about 'What's my purpose?' or 'How do I find my purpose?' My purpose, my purpose.... it feels like there is a lot of pressure and expectation around finding your purpose.

The truth is, when you release and resolve old emotions and beliefs, you liberate your energy and realign with your truth. This realignment allows you to evolve your ideas and fully understand your 'why'.

Suddenly, your purpose is revealed to you, you don't have to find it at all.

You begin working on meaningful projects, you'll be engaged in fulfilling relationships, and focused on creating from a place of inspiration and a true desire to uplift others.

GOOD VIBES ONLY

CHAPTER 5

ACTIVATE YOUR ENERGY THROUGH THE CHAKRA SYSTEM

If you want to find the secrets of the universe, think in terms of energy, frequency and vibration — Nikola Tesla

Energy

Energy is all around us and within us. It's in plants, animals, the earth and the sun. We sense and feel energy, and we increase and expand our energy through our words, thoughts, intentions and actions.

The human body runs on a complex relationship between the physical and the energy body. The energy body contains energy channels known as meridians along which life force energy, or Qi, flows and energy centers, known as chakras.

CHAPTER 5: ACTIVATE YOUR ENERGY THROUGH THE CHAKRA SYSTEM

The Chakras

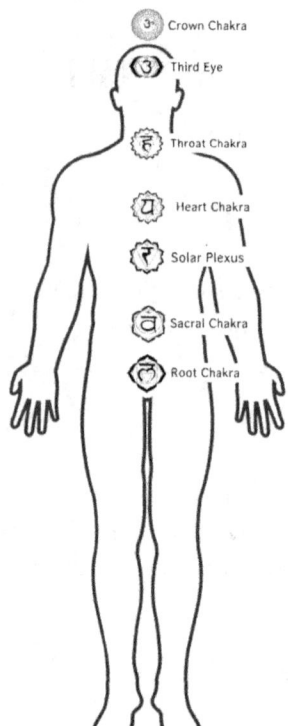

The chakras are like spinning discs or vortexes which send and receive energy, assimilating information and emotions that add to our awareness. Each chakra has its own vibrational rate, resonance and light frequency which gives a color.

We have over 100 chakras, but we commonly focus on the seven major ones. The growing popularity of yoga has assisted with bringing the knowledge of energy and chakras to the mainstream and the seven-chakra system is widely known and used as a framework for increasing awareness and revitalizing the body.

The energy body functions at its optimal rate when the energy is flowing freely, and the chakras are balanced and energized.

- Chakras can be unbalanced or overactive due to too much focus in one area of life.

- They can become blocked or underactive due to trauma, holding on to memories and emotions connected to past events, and

- Lack of positive physical action towards your goals or stagnancy and resistance to change.

Values Levels and Chakras

Now that you have a basic knowledge of the themes at each Values Level and you know which Values Level you are currently experiencing; I want to introduce the correlation between the existential themes of each chakra and the Values Levels.

As I have guided you through the process of resolving rejected levels, I will now show you how to liberate the energy within the corresponding chakra. This will free you to step fully into your personal power and the energy of an ascended leader.

There may be more than one Values Level associated with each of the chakras and each Values Level may be connected to more than one chakra.

If you are familiar with the chakras you may have noticed some correlations between the themes of the chakras and some of the Values Levels. You may also know that energy has a vibration and the higher something vibrates, the more energy it has, and the lighter it appears. Energy, and emotions, either allow or stop us from aligning with ideas, experiences and other people.

There may be more than one Values Level associated with each of the chakras and each Values Level may be connected to more than one chakra. Each chakra is also relevant to a life stage on the physical plane.

Existential themes and life stages of the seven-chakra system

During each stage in our lives, we are working through specific existential themes or challenges that instigate growth and an understanding of how to express ourselves authentically.

Working with your chakras enhances your Values Level resolution as the themes of the chakras correlates to the existential issues

CHAPTER 5: ACTIVATE YOUR ENERGY THROUGH THE CHAKRA SYSTEM

of the Values Levels. It allows you to clear your energy body by releasing stagnant energy and emotions and reframing past events through the eyes of an ascended being.

The Fifth Pillar works with the 12-chakra system, which activates a significant increase in the vibrational rate of the energy body and holistic grounding of intuitive and spiritual information. This is the foundation for cultivating an experience of oneness and transcending the egoic mind, an existential reality predicted at Values Level 8 and beyond.

12-chakra system

The 12-chakra system includes five additional chakras which are said to be the fifth-dimensional chakras (the seven-chakra system being third dimensional). The 12-chakra system is activated through an ongoing commitment to raising your vibrational frequency and meditation to connect with your higher self and your fifth-dimensional aspects.

This is the key to ascending to an even higher level of awareness where intuitive decision making, creative problem solving and making global connections is an automatic response in your daily life.

The Third Pillar of the Ascension Leadership Model focuses on the seven-chakra system to clear and rebalance each of those energy centers, so you become familiar with reading and understanding energy and using it for purposeful creation. It also serves as vital preparation for stepping into the 12-chakra system.

As we go through the existential themes of each chakra, you will begin to get a sense of any aspects of your life which may be connected to an imbalance in a chakra and you may even notice if it is connected to a Values Level which for you requires further resolution. You may also have a sense of any major life events which triggered an imbalance or blockage of energy.

The table below describes the seven major chakras by:

- color
- location in the body
- related existential themes
- life stage in which they are fully developed and the theme related to that life stage, and
- their energetic resonance or vibrational rate
- the Values Level they correspond to is also noted

I have also made a brief note about how you would see blockages or imbalances manifested as behaviors or attitudes in general, and in the context of work or career. Key physical misalignments are also noted.

As you read through the information about the seven-chakra system, notice any feelings or energy in each chakra and consider what emotion it might be connected to.

- Is something within you ready to be healed or released?
- Do you need more of a particular emotion or activity to stimulate this chakra?
- Which chakra can you tune in to, to support you in achieving your goals?

Focus on the aspects of each chakra to energize and balance it.

CHAPTER 5: ACTIVATE YOUR ENERGY THROUGH THE CHAKRA SYSTEM

Chakra	Color	Energetic Theme	Hz
Root or Base located at the base of the spine/perineum	Red	Material issues – success, money, job/career, security. Need for survival. Wealth, accumulation, wealth, status. Physical body, physical energy. Masculine energy and male sexuality. Relationship and connection with tribe or family.	432Hz
Blockages or imbalance in this chakra may manifest as: a lack of money or continuous cycle or 'plenty' to none. Obsession with material possessions. Overly ambitious or career focused with little to no work-life balance. Will do whatever it takes to get a promotion, even at the disadvantage of others. Back pain. Adrenal fatigue. Issues with legs and feet.			
Connected to life stage 0-7 years Awakening our concept of self			
Corresponding Values Levels VL1: Beige – Reactive, biologically driven, survival instinct VL5: Orange – Materialistic, goal directed, self-sufficient, entrepreneurial. Accumulation of wealth.			

Chakra	Color	Energetic Theme	Hz
Sacral located in the lower stomach, just below the navel	Orange	Creative center – fertility, creativity, being in the flow of life. Rituals and traditions. Seat of pleasure – sexuality, sensuality. Indulgence and addiction. Balance. Relationship with others – fitting in with others, being part of a tribe/group. Seeking acceptance.	480Hz

Blockages or imbalance in this chakra may manifest as: Substance abuse and / or addictive behaviors. Feelings of boredom or lack of direction. Under or overactive sex-drive.
Inability to come up with creative or innovative solutions or over complicating a system or business process.
Problems with kidney function. Reproductive issues.

Connected to life stage 8-14 years Understanding we are one with all. Connection to others.

Corresponding Values Level

VL2: Purple – Tribalistic. Group co-operation. Sharing. Safety in numbers.

VL4: Blue - Stability / structure. Meaning and purpose.

CHAPTER 5: ACTIVATE YOUR ENERGY THROUGH THE CHAKRA SYSTEM

Chakra	Color	Energetic Theme	Hz
Solar Plexus located just above and slightly to the right of the navel	Yellow	Centre for personal power – ego, self-esteem, personal will, intellect. Courage, confidence, anxiety, fear, repressed emotions. Ability to assimilate psychic information/ awareness of energy. Ability and willingness to take positive action.	528Hz
Blockages or imbalance in this chakra may manifest as: Anxiety disorders and difficulty socializing. Lack of confidence and low self-esteem. Being on the outer edges of the team or power grabs and backstabbing to advance your own objectives. Digestive and metabolic issues, skin conditions such as Acne.			
Connected to life stage 15-21 years Positivity and knowing who you are			
Corresponding Values Level			
VL3: Red – Power and action. Breaking away from the tribe, asserting the self. Control			

Chakra	Color	Energetic Theme	Hz
Heart located behind the sternum in the center of the chest	Green / Pink	All healing begins here – love, giving and receiving, compassion, empathy, honesty understanding and acceptance. Harmony. Holding on to old emotions – hurt, grief, sadness, loneliness. Putting up barriers. Expressing self-love and love to others (platonic and romantic). Links the physical and spiritual aspects. Blending of masculine and feminine energy.	594Hz

Blockages or imbalance in this chakra may manifest as: Difficulty relating to others. Lack of compassion. Difficulty trusting others.

'Empire building' or underhanded tactics in business.

High blood pressure, lung problems, lingering cough or heavy congestion during or following a cold or flu.

Connected to life stage 22-28 years Devotion to self

Corresponding Values Level

VL6: Green – Love, affiliation. Harmony, acceptance and sensitivity to others.

CHAPTER 5: ACTIVATE YOUR ENERGY THROUGH THE CHAKRA SYSTEM

Chakra	Color	Energetic Theme	Hz
Throat located in the throat	Blue	Centre for self-expression. It is believed a blueprint of the entire body is held here. Right to express self and speak your truth. Authenticity. Communication, sharing, teaching. Listening with respect and compassion. Acceptance for others.	672Hz

Blockages or imbalance in this chakra may manifest as: Feeling stuck. Unable to express yourself freely. Difficulty communicating leading to misunderstandings.

Reluctance to contribute in meetings or to speak up regarding work practices or project directions. Lots of talking but no clear message. Inability to listen or really hear what others are saying.

Neck pain. Sore throat, coughing or losing your voice, earaches.

Connected to life stage 29-35 years Compassion for all

Corresponding Values Level

VL6: Green – Love, affiliation. Harmony, acceptance, and sensitivity to others.

Chakra	Color	Energetic Theme	Hz
Third eye located in the center of the forehead	Purple	Center for insight and intuition – clairvoyance and psychic vision. Insight, perception and intuition. Peace of mind, inner harmony, trusting self. Reasoning, detachment. Vision and acceptance. Faith	720Hz

Blockages or imbalance in this chakra may manifest as: Indecision and inability to gain clarity or understand a situation. Difficulty learning new concepts. Sleep disturbance.

Indecisiveness about business directions. Inability to understand processes and / or identify improvements and efficiency gains.

Feelings of paranoia. Headaches / migraines. Sinus problems.

Connected to life stage 36-42-years Humility and believing in what you do and say.

Corresponding Values Level

VL7: Yellow - Independent. Knowing. Accepting paradoxes.

Chakra	Color	Energetic Theme	Hz
Crown located inside the top of the head towards the back	Violet / White	Connection to Divine – connectedness, wisdom and spiritual purpose. Communion with Divine. Bigger picture, higher consciousness. Inspiration, knowing, intellect/genius. Patience, faith and trust. Mystical experiences, channeling, mediumship, psychic insights.	768Hz

Blockages or imbalance in this chakra may manifest as: Feeling confused, adrift and lacking motivation. Finding it difficult to get excited about things or feel inspired.

Feeling disconnected to work, projects or business objectives.

Feelings of depression. Headaches and / or dizziness.

Connected to life stage 43-49 years Patience

Corresponding Values Level

VL7: Yellow – learns from a variety of sources

VL8: Turquoise – Consciousness, wholistic focus. Comfortable with many paths to knowing.

As you can see, the themes or aspects associated with each chakra relate to different aspects of your life and experiences. By having an awareness of these aspects and working to clear and balance the chakras, you will have the essential energy required to positively work through any situation.

The Fourth Step in the Ascension Leadership Model

The Fourth Step is a chakra clearing protocol that utilizes your intuitive knowing (Pillar 1) and is as easy as tuning in to your 'yes/no.'

By using a basic questioning protocol, you can find out if there are any trapped emotions or stagnant energy in each of your chakras and if it's okay to clear them at this time.

In order to provide a thorough and holistic clearing, I suggest clearing the five major emotions which are very often the root cause of negative patterns of behavior, self-sabotage and diminished feelings of self-worth. These five emotions, if held in the energy centers, can cause significant hindrance to your efforts to make positive changes and move forward, as well as contribute to feelings of tiredness and lethargy, low motivation, and persistent aches and pains. But by clearing them in this specific order, you are releasing that energy for healing, freeing yourself way beyond any previously perceived limitations and opening yourself to unlimited possibilities.

The five major negative emotions are:
1. Anger
2. Sadness
3. Fear
4. Hurt
5. Guilt

The five major negative emotions are:
1. Anger
2. Sadness
3. Fear
4. Hurt
5. Guilt

It's advisable to use the Chakra Clearing Protocol on each of the chakras to clear each of these five emotions when you first work through the Ascension Leadership Model.

By doing so, you are clearing very deeply rooted and long-held energies and liberating that energy so your responses in the future will be unclouded by the illusions of the past. This process will enable you to let go of the burden of carrying the old emotions but will allow you to retain any positive lessons and information that will support you now and into the future.

Later, when you are cycling through the Five Pillars, you can choose to clear the five emotions from each chakra, or you can simply clear 'unforgiveness'.

Unforgiveness

Unforgiveness is the underlying basis for many negative emotions and is either connected to the unforgiveness of self or others. It is often referred to as 'spiritual poison' as it can create significant disharmony and imbalance in our lives. Forgiving yourself or another person does not mean you condone or approve of the behavior or event that caused the unforgiveness. It simply means you no longer carry the emotional and energetic burden connected to it.

ASCENSION LEADERSHIP MODEL STEP 4

Chakra Clearing Protocol

> Set aside some quiet time in a safe and comfortable place for this process. Make sure you can relax and will be uninterrupted.
>
> **Step 1: Decide which chakra you wish to work on during this session.**
>
> - Base
> - Sacral

- Solar Plexus
- Heart
- Throat
- Third Eye
- Crown

Step 2: Take a few deep breaths and tune in to your body. Become aware of any feelings and sensations currently present. Intend and allow your body to relax while affirming that you invite and trust its clear signals.

Step 3: Ask yourself/body-mind if there are any emotions that are ready to be cleared from your chosen chakra.

If you receive a 'yes' response, ask your body-mind if the emotion you need to clear is anger. If you get a 'no' work your way through the list of the five emotions until you get a 'yes'.

Step 4: Once you have identified the specific emotion which is ready to be cleared, ask your body-mind if it is okay to clear, heal and release that emotion from the chakra you are working on today.

Emotional Release Process

At this stage in the process, you need to be very specific with the questions you ask yourself. By being specific, you will ensure a complete release of the emotion and liberation of any trapped energy.

CHAPTER 5: ACTIVATE YOUR ENERGY THROUGH THE CHAKRA SYSTEM

Use these questions:

1. Is this the best time for me to totally clear and release X emotion from X chakra?

2. Are there any other emotions the body-mind would like to clear from this chakra? If you get a 'yes', you don't need to know what other emotions are being cleared as your intuition knows what they are. If you get a 'no', you are only clearing the emotion you identified.

3. Is it possible and safe for this clearing to commence within the next 10 minutes? If 'no', ask up to 60 minutes. Thank the body-mind for giving you a timeframe on when the clearing will commence.

4. When will the emotion of X be totally released and cleared from my X Chakra? (Start from 5-10 minutes after the commencing time.)

5. When you have identified the timeframe when the clearing will be complete, thank your intuition for providing the information and ask, "Are there any positive messages from my Higher Self which will assist me to fully align with my purpose?" If you get a 'yes', set the intention and be willing to and allow this information to come to your conscious mind at a time that is most right for you.

6. Now affirm, "I now allow the total and complete release of X emotion from my X chakra and energy body, through all dimensions and lifetimes and fully activate my x chakra for my highest good."

Now give yourself an opportunity to be still, breathe or meditate to allow the clearing to occur and for your energy body to realign.

You may feel tired after this process, so be gentle with yourself and drink plenty of water. During the process of releasing emotions, and for a time after, you may feel the emotions come to the surface. It's important you don't try to hold the emotion in or ignore it. Allow yourself to recognize and feel it fully so it can be released. You may temporarily re-experience old feelings (good and sad) or experience detailed flashbacks and memories. This may continue until the emotion is fully released from the body.

N.B If the answer is 'no' at question 1, ask the body-mind if clearing this emotion is for the highest good now. If you get a 'yes', go through the protocol again. If you get a 'no' ask your unconscious to provide a positive message connected to that emotion within the next 24-48 hours and then repeat the clearing protocol after that time.

After a clearing process

After a clearing process, you may experience feeling very relaxed and calm, energized, balanced, light and possibly light-headed (in this case, avoid driving, loud environments and stressful situations until it passes).

You may have an increased need to use the bathroom or feel as though you are getting a cold. You may feel emotional or as though you want to cry. These are all signs of release and that your body has accessed the parasympathetic nervous system and is working through the healing process.

You may also notice you sleep for longer or more deeply and have active or bizarre dreams. Dreams are a way for your unconscious mind to transfer information to your conscious mind. If you receive positive messages as a result of clearing a chakra, those messages may come to you through your dreams. Keep a journal or note pad by your bed and jot down the themes, people, or situations in your dreams. Anything recurring or extremely vivid may be a message.

CHAPTER 5: ACTIVATE YOUR ENERGY THROUGH THE CHAKRA SYSTEM

Following a clearing, it's not unusual for you to become more sensitive to certain foods, drinks and products containing unhealthy ingredients or allergens. This is all part of an energetic realignment and is confirmation that you have shifted some energy.

Whatever you experience is exactly right for you. The key is to be gentle with yourself during this process and trust that you are healing and clearing exactly what needs to be healed and cleared at this time for your highest good.

It is possible to clear all five emotions from a chakra in one session depending on how big the shift and energetic response. It can take up to 24 hours for your energy system to adjust, which is why I strongly recommend you wait a minimum of three days before moving on to the next chakra.

If your body-mind only wishes to clear one emotion at a time, wait at least 48 hours before clearing the next emotion. Also, write down anything that comes up after the clearing — memories of past events, bodily sensations, songs, or food cravings. These are also part of the release and insights into positive learnings.

Benefits of clearing negative emotions from your chakras

Over the years I have supported many clients to clear negative emotions from their chakras and energy body. The results I have seen have been varied and at times utterly amazing. Here are a few examples of the positive shifts my clients have reported after using this protocol:

- After releasing anger from her root chakra, Abigail finally sold her house which had been on the market for over 12 months.
- After clearing hurt and guilt from her heart chakra, Wendy reconnected with her sister following 10 years of estrangement.

- Katrina cleared fear and sadness from her crown chakra and began writing children's books.
- When Jessica released the emotions of sadness and fear from her throat chakra and solar plexus, years of recurring throat infections disappeared, and she joined a gospel choir.
- Mia felt stagnant and unmotivated. She cleared hurt and unforgiveness from her root chakra and began trail running. She now competes in national competitions.
- Patricia cleared unforgiveness from her root and sacral chakra. Within six months she had bought a farm and now supplies organic produce to local restaurants.

I can't wait to find out what positive shifts happen for you!

The energy you bring, positive or negative, dictates your perceptions, receptions and radiations — T F Hodge

Low and slow vibrations

The rate of vibration of your energy centers significantly impacts your ability to create results in your work and inspire others. If your vibration is slow and low, you will feel sluggish and stagnant, and others will find it hard to align with your ideas. You may even attract difficult people or unnecessary challenges in your work.

High vibrations

If your vibration is high, you will feel clear, energized and inspired, and others will be attracted to your ideas (this is also dependent on their own Values Levels and their ability to understand the concepts with which you are working).

CHAPTER 5: ACTIVATE YOUR ENERGY THROUGH THE CHAKRA SYSTEM

You will easily be able to clear away obstacles and transcend negativity and have the energy reserves to be agile and flexible in your style. The higher your personal vibration, the more you magnetize and attract what you need into your life. This is the foundational principle for the law of attraction and many ancient healing modalities.

Energetic resonance or the energetic vibration of the bioenergetic system — chakras, auras, meridians — is well documented and has been studied and purposefully applied for thousands of years. Traditional Chinese Medicine (TCM) is among the most notable and comprehensive field of study and practice, with records of working with energy and the meridians dating back to as far as the 3rd century BCE.

TCM works to restore the complementary forces of energy in the body, yin and yang, to create balance and dispel illness and disharmony. This is done via a range of methods including herbal/natural remedies, acupuncture, acupressure, massage and meditation and movement such as Tai Chi and Qi Gong (Chi or Qi meaning energy).

Equally, the ancient Vedic scriptures of India outline a way of life to maintain optimal life force energy and connect with oneness and flow of all that is. The Vedas were written between 1500 and 1000 BCE and speak of meditation, rituals, and medicine to restore and rebalance Prana (energy), health and vitality. Ayurveda is considered an accessory to the fourth book of the Vedas and describes a comprehensive medicine system based on diet, breathwork and yoga.

These traditional practices and ways of life grew from an understanding that everything has an energetic resonance that attracts energy of the same vibrational rate. The ancient Hermetic principle, 'As within, so without', further affirms that as we do the work on ourselves, to clear and enhance our own energy, this will positively reflect on our external experience.

Validation of these age-old understandings of bioenergetics and holistic maintenance of the human system is coming through studies in the field of Quantum physics. In basic terms, Quantum physics describes how particles and atoms make up the Universe. Spoiler alert! It is all created through the movement of energy at the sub-atomic level!

Maintaining a balanced chakra system

After you have worked through the protocol to clear the five major negative emotions from each of your chakras, you will need to maintain that clarity by regularly balancing and expanding your chakras.

> This simple visualization technique is one of the fastest and easiest ways to clear, balance and energize your chakra system and give yourself a boost whenever you need it.
>
> 1. Sit in a comfortable space where you will be undisturbed and bring awareness to your breath.
>
> 2. Visualize and imagine a pure white light above your head.
>
> 3. Breathe that light in through the top of your head and out through the soles of your feet. Feel yourself anchored into the ground.
>
> 4. Now, breathe that light down into your root chakra and see it expanding and turning into a sparkling bright red. Feel a sense of security knowing that you are always safe and protected.

5. Now see that light coming down again through the top of your head and into your sacral chakra. Sense and imagine it growing and expanding, turning to bright orange and feeling a sense of nurturing and creativity expand within your being.

6. Now noticed that light coming down and entering your solar plexus. As it expands within your solar plexus it glows a vibrant yellow gold. Know that it is safe for you to stand in your personal power.

7. Now see the light coming down entering your heart chakra. Feel your heart center opening as waves of love pour through you and from you, filling your chest with a vibrant bright green.

8. The light now enters your throat chakra, expanding and turning to a sparkling color blue. Allowing you to speak your truth.

9. The light now enters your third eye. Bring awareness to the center of your forehead and notice a sense of clarity as the light turns to a vibrant purple.

10. Now see that light expanding and completely filling the top of your head. Your crown chakra opens as you connect with infinite knowledge and divine inspiration.

11. Take a few more moments to imagine the light continuing to expand within and around you, filling your body and lighting up and balancing each chakra – red, orange, yellow, green, blue, purple, ultraviolet.

When I first started to work with energy, I did this visualization every morning. Each time I did it, I got better at concentrating and seeing the colors and I began to notice lots of fun, happy and interesting things happening throughout my day. I just felt better – lighter and more able to hold things lightly. And I loved to wonder what blessings I could attract into my day just by sitting still and imagining colors for ten minutes in the morning!

ASCENSION LEADERSHIP MODEL STEP 5

Raise your Energetic Vibration

Your energy level is affected by the food you eat, the people you interact with and the environment you are in. It is also affected by the things you watch on the television or see on social media, the music you listen to, and the biochemical substances in your cleaning products, cosmetics, and environment.

As you already understand, everything is energy and energy is everywhere. When you work through Step 4 of the ALM and release negative emotions from your chakras and regularly do the visualization to balance them, you will go a long way to raising the vibration of your energy body. This in turn may make you more sensitive to external influences but will ensure you are always clear and able to connect with your intuition and psychophysical signals in order to discern information and receive guidance.

Exercises

There are many ways to raise your energetic vibration and you will notice when you feel you need a 'tune-up'. Here I have suggested a few simple things you can do to maintain clear energy and raise your vibration.

1. **Reduce or eliminate additives and chemicals** from your diet and beauty regime. As I mentioned before, I make no recommendations for a specific diet to follow and I encourage you to be guided by what your body is telling you. I can, however, tell you that additives such as food

colors, preservatives, flavor enhancers and emulsifiers are not compatible with the human body.

In my work I use a TCM muscle monitoring technique to help identify food sensitivities which cause inflammation, allergies, and low energy. Foods with these ingredients are always the culprit. There is lots of evidence-based information about food additives to avoid, so do your research and find out what you need to know to help you reduce or eliminate the consumption of these chemicals.

2. **Media detox**. This is not a new concept and we are often encouraged to turn off our phones for a day to get some peace and relax. There are many benefits to this including having less contact with EMF emitting devices. Electro and Magnetic Fields (EMF) are invisible radiations emitted from our computers, phones, televisions, microwaves, power lines and other electrical devices. Too much exposure can act like static in our own energy field and cause us to feel flat, tired, irritable, scattered, or find it difficult to clearly connect with our intuition.

The other beneficial aspect of a media detox is reduced exposure to the drama and trauma of the 24-hour news cycle, contrived, over-emotional reality shows and the endless feed of negativity and judgmental commentary of social media.

Bill Hicks once said, "Watching television is like taking a can of black spray paint to your third eye." I fully concur and apply this to social media also. Protect your energy and reduce the amount of television you watch, purge your social feeds of negative people or even just the volume of unnecessary 'noise' in your feed and make regular time to read inspiring books, or spend time with people who uplift and support you.

3. **Spend time in nature.** Being in natural environments is an amazing way to clear your energy body and raise your vibration. This can be as simple as:

   a. swimming in the ocean

   b. anchoring your feet into the sand

   c. sitting in your garden and recharging in the sun, or

   d. taking yourself away to a forest or woodland to meditate and connect with the energy of the trees, birds and elementals.

4. **Cut energetic cords** of attachment and call back your energy. We form energetic connections with every single person we ever meet. In the Huna healing tradition, these cords are called Aka connections and they hold us back from personal growth and stepping into our magnificence. The more interaction we have with a person, the stronger these connections become.

   Energetic cords connect you to another person via the energy body and draw energy away from you, feeding the other person and reinforcing the connection and their beliefs, attitudes and opinions about you (as you do for them). Even if you haven't seen them for years and don't even think about them anymore, if you do not cut the cord, it will still be present. You can also be energetically connected to a place or a past event.

Cutting cords

The simplest way to cut cords of connection is to find a space where you will be undisturbed, relax and breathe deeply.

Step 1: Close your eyes and sense and feel the cords around your body, they're often connected to the heart chakra, solar plexus and sacral chakras. The cords may appear like thin strands or like thick tubes or rope.

Step 2: Set the intention and ask your Higher Self to assist with releasing people, places or things that are connected to you for their own highest good and recalling your energy for your ultimate ascension.

Step 3: Imagine yourself cutting these cords with golden scissors or a shining sword. Send loving energy along the cords as they return to the other person and know that this is for the highest good of all. Notice as these cords fall away and completely dissolve, bringing back your energy to yourself and healing the space where they were once connected.

Step 4: As you are finishing this process affirm, "I now call back my energy through all dimensions of time and space, all past lifetimes and from all people places and events, to be returned to my Being." Take a few more moments to breathe, relax and receive. When you feel ready, open your eyes and notice you feel energized and clear.

Cutting the cords of attachment does not mean that the person will no longer be in your life, it merely means that you will no longer be restricted by old perceptions and negative energetic bonds.

These few simple techniques will ensure your energy is always vibrating at the highest rate possible. With regular maintenance, your energy body will feel more vibrant, have increased mental clarity and creativity, and be highly tuned in to the messages and guidance from your intuition.

Rachel's story

Rachel came to see me because she was having trouble with her ex.

They always had a strained relationship and just lately things were becoming very difficult. She was finding it hard to manage visitation with the kids and he regularly failed to pay maintenance. Each time she spoke with him she had a tense feeling in her chest and stomach. We worked through the chakra clearing protocol to release feelings of anger and unforgiveness from her root chakra and solar plexus. After a few weeks, she reported her ex had started making the regular payments, however, she was still finding it hard to communicate with him as he kept bringing up issues from the past.

I talked to her about the theory of energetic cords and she confirmed she felt drained and tired when she thought of or spoke to, her ex-husband. I guided her through a cord-cutting process, asking her to send love and healing to her ex-husband so that he might move forward in his life and find happiness. I then asked her to imagine love and healing coming back to her, filling the space where the cord once was, allowing her to know that she too deserved happiness and the freedom to move forward in life.

Rachel reported during the session that her whole body was tingling, particularly her hands and feet. She said she was feeling a swirling sensation in her head, which was not unpleasant, but it was intense, and it took some time for the feeling to dissipate.

CHAPTER 5: ACTIVATE YOUR ENERGY THROUGH THE CHAKRA SYSTEM

At her next session, she told me that out-of-the-blue her ex-husband had called her and apologized for being so difficult recently. He revealed he was going through some changes and was taking it out on her because that's what he always used to do. He agreed to be more open to custody arrangements and to communicate with her regularly about visitation and maintenance. He also said he hoped she found a new partner who would be kind to her and the kids.

CHAPTER 6

YOUR UNLIMITED LEADERSHIP POTENTIAL

Live the Life of Your Dreams: Be brave enough to live the life of your dreams according to your vision and purpose instead of the expectations and opinions of others.
— Roy T. Bennett, The Light in the Heart

It's important for you to understand how powerful you really are. We have all heard the famous saying of Napoleon Hill, "What the mind can conceive and believe, it can achieve." There is so much truth to this, and it comes from a deep understanding that our ideas and beliefs about ourselves, our ability and the world around us, is greatly impacted by what we think about and believe or accept to be true.

Emma's story

Emma had been working in the same team for eight years and she was beginning to feel stagnant. She wanted to progress into a more senior role, but she always seemed to get overlooked when opportunities arose. We worked together and resolved some lingering attitudes associated with VL4 thinking and she worked on releasing old emotions of hurt and resentment.

After our first few sessions, she told me she had noticed that when she was getting ready for work, she was thinking about how boring it would be, how no one valued her, and that she thought the manager was 'uppity'. It was then she realized, she was the one blocking her progression due to her thoughts and beliefs and 'generally icky energy'. We worked together to create a specific intention for her career and to reframe her views of her current situation. She wanted to be in a new and engaging role within six months and have an improved relationship with her manager.

Emma began telling herself there were lots of interesting aspects of her current work and, as she was the only one trained to do that work, her contribution to the team and was highly valued. She saw herself making genuine connections with her team members and connected to good feelings when she thought about going into the office. She started to look at her manager in a different way and see that her manager had a different communication style to hers, but there were many things they had in common and could easily talk about.

The more Emma told herself she was valued; the more interesting work came her way. She was even given the opportunity to work on a project with her manager and that really helped her to identify better ways for them to communicate. Things were improving, and then an opportunity to act in a senior role for six months came up. She was not chosen.

A colleague from another section was given the role. Emma could not understand. She was fuming because the person who got the job didn't have as much experience as she did, and she really thought she was making great connections with everyone in her team. We dug a little deeper and discovered that when the senior role came up, Emma didn't make it clear she was interested. She told her manager she didn't mind who got the job. When I asked her why she realized it was because she was afraid of not being able to 'cut the mustard'. Emma knew what she had to do next.

She set to work releasing feelings of unworthiness or not being good enough and worked to balance and energize her solar plexus. She wanted to connect with her confidence and courage. She started imagining walking into her manager's office and telling her she wanted a promotion and some new projects. In this inner scene, her manager eagerly obliged. Emma began reviewing her career successes and building evidence of her abilities and value.

A few weeks later she felt confident and that the timing was right. She scheduled a meeting with her manager and prepared some notes. Emma told her manager she felt she could have easily done the senior role and that she would like to move into higher duties. She outlined her experience and performance record and suggested a few special projects that she could lead and who she would like on the project team. Emma then told her manager that she knew if she was more assertive about her desires to progress within the team, she would have been considered for that senior role. Long story short, Emma was promoted to Senior Project Manager and given three team members to lead in the design and implementation of high-value public infrastructure projects. She even got to present one of her projects as an example of best practice at a national conference.

Once Emma identified the negative story she was telling herself and saw the hidden beliefs that were keeping her stuck, she created a new story. She *conceived* a more exciting job and took responsibility for upgrading her thoughts and energy, she began to *believe* she was capable and worthy and within six months, she *achieved*.

The Second Pillar of the Ascension Leadership Model deals with beliefs and attitudes through the Values Levels and, as you will experience, after resolving your highly rejected Values Levels, the world around you will shift according to your thinking.

CHAPTER 6: YOUR UNLIMITED LEADERSHIP POTENTIAL

The key to unlocking your unlimited leadership potential lies in regularly reviewing your beliefs and goals and reframing anything that does not support you to achieve your ultimate vision.

In my work with other leaders, I always take the view that a client will not actualize any change or positive results if I do not believe she can.

The world around me will always reflect what I think about it. If I believe you have unlimited potential, then the work we do together will reveal that. Of course, you must also believe you have unlimited potential, and sometimes it takes a little bit of work to uncover and release anything that might be stopping you from truly, at your deepest level, believing that too (see Step 4).

Your beliefs about yourself are learned and integrated at a very early age. They are shaped by your family, your environment, your education, culture, religion, TV shows you watch, and the advertising around you. Your unconscious mind takes in everything you have ever experienced and sorts it in a way that influences your behaviors, responses, and attitudes in later years.

Your unconscious mind even interprets those experiences based on what you already know and believe; it sorts and categorizes them based on familiar emotional responses and situations.

Another important thing to know about your unconscious mind is that it very often takes things personally. Even the little things. So, a blank look from a colleague who is having a bad day might be interpreted by your unconscious as a sign that they don't like you. Cue the inner monologue "OMG what did I do, did I say something to offend her, am I too this or that? Blah blah blah," until you get yourself all worked up over nothing more than an expression on the face of someone who was lost deep in their own thoughts. They may not even have noticed you were there at all!

Not only does the unconscious mind take things personally, but it also really wants to please you in the easiest and quickest way possible. Knowing this can be very useful if you're watchful of your thoughts and specific in your instructions. Knowing how to effectively employ the unconscious mind in the purposeful creation of your experience is the basis of the Fourth Pillar of the Ascension Leadership Model.

Intention

- What is your intention for reading this book?
- What do you intend to do with the knowledge?
- What do you intend to do in your work or career?
- As a leader, what is your intent for stepping into your personal power?

Your intention is essentially your 'why' and your purpose for doing the work that you do, interacting with people the way that you do, and creating the experiences that give you a sense of fulfillment.

When you become clear on your intentions (you're 'why'), you will become clear in your communications, actions and strategies to get there. Your unconscious mind will find ways to bring the perfect circumstances to you to help fulfill your intention because your unconscious mind will now recognize that you are consciously aligned with your purpose and are willing to be guided and take action.

CHAPTER 6: YOUR UNLIMITED LEADERSHIP POTENTIAL

Kathryn and Olivier's story

Kathryn and Olivier were cousins who grew up as though they were sisters. They lived near each other, had the same interests, and went to the same college. As they were nearing graduation, they were planning their next steps. They had both always talked about traveling together and thought it would be a nice break after so much studying.

Kathryn was excited and began looking up places to visit, flights and transfers, things to do, and what to see. She knew that seeing the world would give her inspiration for meaningful ways to use her qualifications and the confidence to find her perfect career. She told her parents she would leave in July for four weeks. When she met with Olivier and told her what she had planned, Olivier just said she would go along with whatever Kathryn had in mind. The more research Kathryn did, the more excited she got. She picked up some extra shifts at work, saved as much money as she could and often declined nights out so she could work and earn more travel money. Olivier just continued as usual, enjoying socializing, studying for her finals, and relaxing on weekends.

The week before graduation Kathryn told Olivier it was time to book their air tickets and some accommodation. She showed Olivier the travel plan she had put together, neatly curated in a journal with pictures of the places they would visit and notes on local experiences and traditional cafes and markets to explore.

Olivier then realized she didn't have enough money for the flights, let alone the accommodation or spending money. She told Kathryn she couldn't go. Kathryn was pretty bummed out because she had put so much effort and energy into planning a wonderful adventure and she didn't want to go alone. She thought about it for days, she really wanted to go but knew she'd have more fun and be more inspired if she were with a friend. Every day until graduation she looked at her travel journal and the pictures of all the places she wanted to visit – the Eiffel Tower, the Colosseum, Sagrada Família. She felt so inspired when she looked at these pictures but thought she would have to wait until Olivier was ready.

A week after graduation Kathryn ran into an old high school friend who had just graduated from a different college and was home visiting her parents. They talked about their studies and their career plans and Kathryn told her about her plans to travel to Europe, but that she could not go because Olivier wasn't ready. Her friend looked excited and told Kathryn her sister had booked a tour around Europe with a group of her friends and was now unable to go because she had gotten a promotion and needed to start immediately. Her sister didn't know what to do with the ticket as it was non-refundable and asked Kathryn if she would like to buy it. Before Kathryn knew the words were coming out of her mouth she was saying, "Yes! Yes! Yes!" The tour left in July for four weeks and included all the places on Kathryn's list. She had so much fun with the other girls on the tour and she began to see all the wonderful ways she could use her qualifications to start a meaningful career. She began making a list in her journal of all the places she would apply to when she returned home.

Reticular Activating System

There is a small piece of the brain called the Reticular Activating System (RAS) which acts as a filter for all the sensory data you experience throughout the day. The RAS filters this data to make sure you don't get overloaded with information and, crucially, selects the most important information for you to become consciously aware of.

The importance of the data the RAS chooses is based on how that information will serve you, e.g. is it for your survival, your education or personal development, will it help you achieve your goals and fulfill your intentions. So, if you use mental rehearsal, visualization, vision boards or affirmations, you are training the RAS to be on the lookout for the information that will get you what you want.

When others understand your intention for leading the organization in a particular direction or developing new ideas, strategies and products, they can more easily identify an alignment within themselves.

The same is true with your colleagues. When others understand your intention for leading the organization in a particular direction or developing new ideas, strategies and products, they can more easily identify an alignment within themselves. When they see your purpose, they will feel your passion and they will then willingly support you in the achievement of your desired outcomes. No longer just working in a job, your colleagues will be connected to the vision and will find greater meaning and fulfillment in the work they do with you. The energetic alignment of everyone involved synchronizes and increases in response to the group's shared willingness to support the goal.

An effective leader sets clear intentions

To be an effective leader, you need to set very clear intentions to understand your purpose and why you are doing what you do. Setting intentions is like creating your future. You can reverse engineer by starting with the ideal outcome. Start with the end goal and then be open to receive the intuitive and unconscious guidance to lead you to that outcome.

To be an effective leader, you need to set very clear intentions to understand your purpose and why you are doing what you do. Setting intentions is like creating your future.

You see, another thing about the unconscious mind is that it doesn't differentiate between memories and imagination. Biologically, something you experience and observe with your eyes travels through the brain from the occipital lobe to the parietal lobe which then forms a memory of that experience.

Whereas something you imagine flows in the opposite direction – parietal lobe to occipital lobe. Because the location of the brain activity or neural signals is the same, the unconscious mind will associate the visualization with an emotional response and maybe even connect it to other similar events and catalog it in much the same way it catalogs actual memories.

The occipital lobe deals with visual information, the things you see — light, shadows, movement, and depth perception — and the parietal lobe deals with other sensory data such as touch, smell and taste. Knowing this means creative visualization or mental rehearsing is one of the most powerful tools you can use to assist you to move towards your goals.

The more you practice creating a future memory, the more the unconscious mind can be aware of opportunities and actions that will help you attain it. The key to using visualization to its fullest potential is creating the vision in such detail, with such clarity, that you can see, hear, feel and smell every aspect of that desired experience. Make the image as big and bright and dynamic as you can. Breathe life into it and notice all the details.

You can visualize any positive outcomes you wish to achieve, such as a successful job interview, a romantic date, a happy social occasion, a confident presentation. But more powerfully, you can visualize and mentally rehearse a significant, positive outcome of your work as an ascended, intuitive leader.

CHAPTER 6: YOUR UNLIMITED LEADERSHIP POTENTIAL

ASCENSION LEADERSHIP MODEL STEP 6

Uncover your purpose and create your future

This is the step where you repeatedly ask yourself 'why'. Book some time in your calendar, set up a meeting with yourself, do whatever it takes to create the time and space to uncover your purpose.

- Why do you do the work you do?
- What is the purpose of your work?
- Who does it impact and how does that serve you?
- What is the highest intention of your work?

Keep asking yourself these questions until you have a very clear understanding of how your work helps you fulfill *your* purpose.

Helping others is noble, but how does that create meaning for you? How does it serve you?

> Here's a simple process that helps start to uncover the path to your purpose. If you feel guided to delve deeper into this process, please contact me directly at hello@theleader-within.com and we can chat personally.

Finding my purpose flow chart

> I'm writing a book.

Why?

> To tell women about the Ascension Leadership Model.

Why?

> So, they can reconnect to their intuition.

Why, what does that do for them?

> Supports them to have confidence in their intuition so they can fulfill their purpose.

How does that serve me?

> Enables me to share my knowledge and connect with many people.

How does that fulfill my purpose?

> The book is a vehicle for teaching universal truths and connection to all that is.

Does this mean your purpose is centered around teaching?

> Yes, my purpose is to share the knowledge to help others Ascend.

CHAPTER 6: YOUR UNLIMITED LEADERSHIP POTENTIAL

My gift to you

> Download a complimentary blank "Finding My Purpose" template at www.theleader-within.com

Working through a simple process like this will answer many of your 'whys' and help to uncover your purpose. Our life purpose can't always be filtered down to a single word, nor should it be. But this process will help you to get closer to your reason for being. In working through this process, you may also have identified some key goals or milestones. They are the goals you are going to include when you create your future.

Create your future

The second part of Step 6 of the Ascension Leadership Model is the creation of the future you deserve and desire.

> Having now identified why you are doing what you do and some key goals around that, I want you to now picture your most desired and ideal outcome. Make a very clear picture of a moment that represents the achievement of that goal or fulfillment of that desire. You are going to turn that into a future memory.
>
> **Here's how**
> - Find a quiet space where you will be comfortable and uninterrupted, take a few deep breaths, and relax your body. Bring awareness to any sensations within the body and set the intention to create your ideal future in this moment.

- Relaxing even more deeply, project your energy to that moment in time where the fulfillment of this goal is most appropriate (one week, three months, one year).

- See that point in time and hover above it, noticing how bright that moment in time is and the energy that is radiating from that moment.

- Now bring to mind that very clear picture of your goal or outcome and see every tiny intricate detail of that picture. Look through your own eyes, notice where you are, who you are with and the activity going on around you. Hear the voices of the other people (if there are others with you) and the sounds around you. Notice the temperature of the space you are in, or the breeze or warmth from the sun if you are outdoors. See, hear, smell and touch every single detail of that moment. Make the image clearer and the colors brighter.

- Become aware of your emotions and internal state. Feel those feelings of excitement, pride, joy, or happiness at having achieved your goal. Feel the energy within you as you affirm you have succeeded.

- Take a moment to bask in those beautiful feelings as the colors and sounds and smells are amplified, the picture becoming more and more real as if you are right there in that moment now.

- Now take a photo in your mind and look at that photo. See yourself in that photo, having achieved your goal, looking so joyful and proud, embedded in that scene. Again, notice any people, furniture, trees, or other details and make the colors brighter.

- Looking at that photo, send to yourself and everything in the picture a stream of loving, high vibrational energy. See the energy pouring from your heart into the photo as it is filled with vitality and life.

- Take a few more deep breaths and continue sending love and energy to the image for as long as you wish, knowing that you have already achieved this goal.

- When the image is completely filled with life-force energy, drop the photo and watch as it gently floats down into the bright light of the moment in time you have chosen for the fulfillment of this goal. Watch as it floats down and lands exactly at that perfect point in time and notice how every moment surrounding it becomes brighter and brighter too, lining up to support you in the achievement of your goal.

- Notice that light getting brighter and brighter, expanding until it fully surrounds you and infuses you. See the light expanding out beyond the bounds of the Universe.

- Know in this moment that you are totally loved and protected, and you are the creator of your perfect reality.

- When you are ready, take a few more deep breaths and open your eyes.

I bet you feel amazing right now!

You have just created a future memory

Your unconscious mind will file that future memory in the same way as it creates and files all memories and you will now find things around you shifting and aligning to support you in the achievement of that goal.

You can do that exercise as many times as you like and for any situation that you wish. Remember to charge your future memory full of positive feelings and life-force energy and know that whatever you can conceive and believe, you can achieve.

CHAPTER 7

ASCEND BEYOND NOW – STEPPING INTO THE 12-CHAKRA SYSTEM

The Fifth Pillar of the Ascension Leadership Model is Activation to support your continuous growth and learning.

Our personal evolution never stops, and we are always shifting and changing aspects of ourselves and our experience. Once you have followed the steps in the Ascension Leadership Model and completed the processes to tune into your intuition, transcend Values Levels, raise your vibration, and set purposeful intentions for your work and your role as a leader, you must now commit to taking positive actions to realize your vision.

By using meditation as the key technique for achieving this pillar, and a vehicle for continued ascension, you can further expand your energy and activate your fifth-dimensional chakras to access universal knowledge and all your wisdom and experience through every incarnation your soul has experienced.

Our personal evolution never stops, and we are always shifting and changing aspects of ourselves and our experience.

Do I really have to meditate?

'Blurgh. Do I really have to meditate? I haven't got time, can't sit still, don't have the right space, have too much to think about, what if I can't do it properly...' Yep, that was me.

CHAPTER 7: ASCEND BEYOND NOW – STEPPING INTO THE 12-CHAKRA SYSTEM

Heaps of excuses why I couldn't meditate, but one very powerful reason why I needed to. It was the only thing that was going to help me focus and really connect with my intuition and purpose. I'd seen all the images of monks on mountain tops and heard the tales of totally Zen dudes sitting crossed legged for hours while their incense burns in the background. I knew I wasn't able to do that, but I just had to start trying a few different approaches until I found something that worked for me. Clearing my mind – tough and very noisy! Chanting – I was way too self-conscious for that. Focusing on my breath – better. It made it easier to let thoughts come in and then blow them away. Guided meditation – a good place to get used to the process.

I found a very basic color meditation and worked with that for a while (see Step 4). Essentially, you just inhale white light through the top of your head and exhale colors through each chakra – red at the root chakra, orange at the sacral chakra, yellow at the solar plexus, green at the heart, blue at the throat, purple at the third eye and violet at the crown. That simple chakra balance and meditation really got me back on-line with energy and presence and self-awareness. It provided a very simple way for me to stay in the moment while noticing what was happening on the inside. It only took 10 minutes and I could do it sitting in a chair or lying in bed or in the park on my lunch break. And every time I did it, I felt great!

From there I started experimenting with some different styles and have found that over time, I just naturally fell into my own process. For me meditation is as simple as this:

- I light a candle and sit in a comfortable chair.
- I stare into the candle for 3-5 breaths and allow my eyes to gently close. I imagine the light of the candle expanding inside me and with each exhale all thoughts, worries, aches, pains or stress is pushed outside of my body.

- Once the light has cleared my body and fully expanded, I bring my attention to my heart, my throat and my head. I acknowledge and accept multiple possibilities and unlimited potentials and I notice the ripples and vibrations in those areas and connect to the feeling of lightness and joy they bring.

- I sit in that energy for as long as I wish.

- When I open my eyes, I feel refreshed, lighter, and more focused. I also feel, hear and see my inner guidance with so much clarity. I'm deeply connected to Universal Consciousness!

the whole point of the Ascension Leadership Model is to give you a process to enable you to quickly make effective decisions that will have multiple and significant positive benefits on a massive scale.

Sounds a bit out there I know, but the whole point of the Ascension Leadership Model is to give you a process to enable you to quickly make effective decisions that will have multiple and significant positive benefits on a massive scale. By strengthening the connection between your cognitive and creative brain, tuning into subtle energies, and viewing the world from a broader perspective, you are doing just that. You are clearing the way to increased productivity and efficiency, reduced stress, and greater creativity and enhanced perception. You are fine-tuning your system to such a degree that you will always have clear knowingness.

Commitment to Ascension

In Chapter 5 I briefly mentioned the 12-chakra system and the five additional chakras which are known as the fifth-dimensional chakras. These chakras are present in everyone but are dormant as we don't need them to function in our everyday experience. When you clear and balance the seven-chakra system, you prepare the energy body for the fifth-dimensional chakra activation by raising your vibration and clearing away illusions about yourself and the world around you.

When you do this, you begin to perceive energy more clearly and understand the subtleties which reveal the truth of a person or situation. This awareness and higher vibrational rate prepare your energy body for the activation of your dormant chakras.

The 12-chakra system

This system is activated through meditation and maintaining harmony in your energy body. These fifth-dimensional chakras awaken positive aspects within yourself that enable you to perceive the world in truth and move through it with grace and compassion. They anchor your ultimate potential and inner wisdom and strengthen your connection to all that is.

Characteristics of the fifth-dimensional chakras

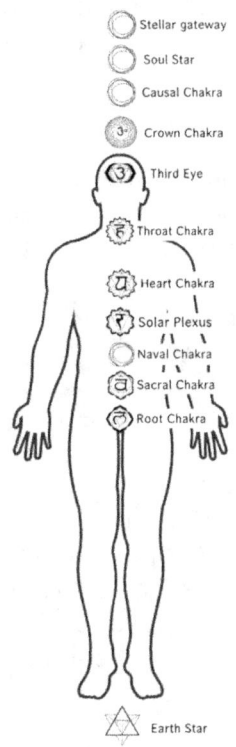

The Earth Star Chakra

This chakra is located below the feet and anchors you fully into the earth's energy, grounding your intentions and supercharging your motivation and ability to create your experience. It holds your ultimate potential for this lifetime and enables you to work with the fifth-dimensional energy in a way that is most supportive of your intentions.

The earth star chakra is the first of the fifth-dimensional chakras to become activated and when it is, you reach a new level of self-acceptance and of feeling comfortable in any situation. It is totally grounding, which means you no longer have to ground yourself in ways that you might for the seven-chakra system. This chakra is black and white and as it is beginning to activate you will feel tingling or an increased sensation in the soles of your feet.

The Naval Chakra

This chakra is located just above the third-dimensional sacral chakra and connects you to a greater level of creativity and manifestation. When the naval chakra is activated, others are drawn to your warmth and calming presence. You instantaneously create harmonious relationships and inspire others. This chakra is a vibrant orange color and will draw new souls towards you if it is for your highest good.

The Causal Chakra

This chakra is above and to the back of your head. It is connected to Moon energy and is the first of the three chakras above your third-dimensional crown chakra.

When the causal chakra is activated, your spiritual connection is greatly enhanced, and your intuitive abilities significantly increase. You develop the ability to see the connections between all things and to perceive and fully understand a situation in moments. The activation of this chakra will bring you a sense of deep inner peace and the ability to remain unaffected by drama around you. It is pure bright white.

The Soul Star Chakra

This chakra is located about one foot above your head and connects you to your soul energy and all your wisdom through all your incarnations. When it is activated you are able to source any information required to support your intentions. The soul star chakra reminds you of your inherent gifts and purpose, and of your ancestral karma. It enables you to understand yourself at a soul level. It is a magenta color with hints of blue.

The Stellar Gateway

The stellar gateway chakra is located one meter (or just over three feet) above your head and strengthens your connection to your Higher Self and All That Is.

When the stellar gateway is activated and fully open, you have access to the unlimited light and high-frequency energy of the Universe. It is oneness. The stellar gateway radiates a golden light into you and all around you.

I'm sure you can already see the benefit of activating the fifth-dimensional chakras and the possibilities this opens to you as a leader and in your personal life.

In terms of energetic alignment with the Values Levels, activating these chakras means:

- You actualize a level of thinking which is beyond your own self-interests and act from a place of global perspective and benefits for all.
- You have resolved your personal issues with survival, supply, self-worth, and needing to conform, comply, fit in and or submit.
- You no longer need the acceptance of others or the external validation of structures, systems, society.
- Your motivation is purpose-driven, your purpose is connection driven and your connection is evident in all your work.

The Fifth Pillar of the ALM is meditation and put simply, meditation is ascension.

There have been thousands of studies into the benefits of meditation and you probably have already at least tried to meditate, or maybe you already have a regular practice.

Meditation has been shown to:
- improve sleep
- increase productivity
- reduce stress and
- improve mental health and well-being.

The benefits of meditation are far-reaching, and it has now come to the center in many large organizations, being taught to CEOs and encouraged among employees. For a long time, celebrities

CHAPTER 7: ASCEND BEYOND NOW – STEPPING INTO THE 12-CHAKRA SYSTEM

and athletes have been talking about meditation, and workplace mindfulness programs are not uncommon today.

But please don't get concerned. Meditation is not sitting still in an awkward position for hours on end, clearing the mind and becoming Zen. That's only one type of meditation, but it's one more suited to monks and gurus and perhaps not the best fit for busy folk like you and me.

It's important also to understand that mindfulness is not meditation either. Mindfulness is more about directing your focus, being very aware of an activity and taking each step with purpose. It is useful for prompting us to stop and take a breath, to slow down and to let go of the stresses of the moment, but meditation is even more than that.

So what is meditation?

Meditation provides a way to connect the left and right hemispheres of the brain so the creative and cognitive operate in unison. The process boosts your potential by increasing your ability to adapt to change and perceive everything in an instant.

Let's start to answer that question with what meditation is not.

One of the biggest myths about meditation is that you must clear the mind and be very still for a long period of time. I feel that is why so many of us think we are not good at meditation. Yes, there are meditation styles that require stillness and a clear mind, but meditation is more active and achievable for regular people.

Meditation provides a way to connect the left and right hemispheres of the brain so the creative and cognitive operate in unison. The process boosts your potential by increasing your ability to adapt to change and perceive everything in an instant. The more you meditate, the greater the connection of your brain.

Here's the science.

The corpus callosum is a band of nerves that runs down the middle of the brain like a bridge, connecting the left and right hemispheres. It allows information to pass from one side to the other, integrating motor (co-ordination) sensory and cognitive functions.

A lot of information crosses this bridge in every moment and, as you can imagine, the capacity of the bridge dictates the efficiency of the brain. The corpus callosum is made up of around 200 million nerve fibers and is approximately 10cm in length. It finishes developing by the time you are 12 years old.

Unless……

Meditation provides a way of biohacking the brain to increase the size of the corpus callosum. The more often you meditate, the stronger that bridge becomes and the quicker your left and right brain hemispheres communicate. This enables you to reduce the 'noise' in your head and enter a state of calm so you can adapt to change and switch into creative and intuitive problem-solving.

All the demands and challenges faced by a leader can be met through regular meditation. And by regular I don't mean something you have to find time in your busy schedule to do, another task that adds stress to your day or reason to beat yourself up if you didn't get to it or stick with it.

I mean discovering something you look forward to every day and easily integrate into your self-care regime. By prioritizing time to access a state that activates your energy centers, increases your compassion, creativity, intuition and purposefulness, you are connecting deeply to the leader within.

CHAPTER 7: ASCEND BEYOND NOW – STEPPING INTO THE 12-CHAKRA SYSTEM

Ascension Leadership Model Step 7

Meditation to Activate the 12-Chakra System

This simple meditation uses a visualization technique to access the golden Mahatma energy to activate the 12-chakra system. This energy is believed to be the most important energy available to us for expansion and ascension. It provides a direct link between us and Universal Consciousness and is of the highest, purest vibration.

This meditation also calls forth your personal Merkabah Star. Your Merkabah looks like two intersecting pyramids with each section spinning in opposite directions. It draws feminine energy up from the earth and masculine energy down from the heavens to create perfect balance and harmony. It also provides your consciousness with protection and transport to higher dimensions.

I strongly recommend doing this meditation every day for three weeks to fully open and activate the fifth-dimensional chakras and integrate the high-frequency Mahatma energy into the third-dimensional chakras.

After three weeks, it can be done weekly, or whenever you feel the need. For a complimentary guided recording of this meditation visit www.theleader-within.com

---

Find a space where you can be comfortable and uninterrupted. Sit in a chair with your feet on the ground or lay down allowing your spine to straighten and relax.

Close your eyes and take deep, comfortable breaths. Notice every sensation in your body – hands, feet, chest, head. Set the intention to connect with the high vibrational golden Mahatma energy for the activation of your fifth-dimensional chakras.

Relax and continue to breathe.

Visualize a vibrant ball of golden light. Imagine that light expanding all around you. Now notice an intensely glowing Merkabah Star above your head. Become aware of the beautiful golden high vibrational energy of that star and the golden column of light it radiates onto you.

Ask your Higher Self to help you assimilate and integrate this energy for the activation of your 12-chakra system. Feel yourself connecting with the golden Mahatma energy and open yourself to the activation process.

See the Merkabah Star above your head and notice as it connects a column of golden light through you and right down into the Earth. Feel the golden light traveling down to the soles of your feet and see an explosion of Mahatma energy as your earth star chakra is now fully opened and activated, anchoring you into the Earth's energy and grounding your intentions.

You are now supported by the Earth's energy and connected with your ultimate potential. As you fully accept your role as a creator and you align with your highest purpose, you see your earth star chakra turning to a shining black and white.

CHAPTER 7: ASCEND BEYOND NOW – STEPPING INTO THE 12-CHAKRA SYSTEM

The golden light now travels up into your root chakra, cleansing, clearing, and upgrading your root chakra to the fifth-dimensional vibration, connecting you to a sense of stability and safety, knowing all your needs are met in every moment. Your root chakra now glows sparkling platinum.

As the golden energy continues up into your sacral chakra, clearing and realigning you to the high vibrational fifth-dimension energy, your sacral chakra transmutes into a glowing pink and all energetic cords of attachment are dissolved for the highest good of all. You feel a wave of complete harmony wash over you.

You now see the light flow into your stomach and notice your fifth-dimensional naval chakra activating and opening, exploding into life with Mahatma energy. See your navel chakra fully activated, allowing you to connect with all that is. See this chakra turn to a vibrant orange as you fully align to a greater level of creativity and manifestation.

Now see the energy ascending into your solar plexus, allowing you to feel completely at peace, trusting in your Soul knowledge. Thank your Higher Self for allowing this fifth-dimensional energy to gently integrate into your solar plexus as it glows a bright golden light opening you gracefully to your personal power.

See that golden light filling your heart chakra. See your heart chakra as a pure white 33 petaled rose which now fully opens and expands as the fifth-dimensional energy connects you to the cosmic heart, immersing you in the energy of healing, compassion and pure joy.

The Mahatma energy now enters your throat chakra. As it clears and purifies your throat chakra, you are connected to your truest self and fifth-dimensional energy aligns your communication and self-expression. Your third-dimensional throat chakra is now transformed into the fifth-dimensional glowing royal blue, all your communications now come from a place of loving acceptance and compassion.

Visualize the golden light entering your third eye as it clears away third-dimensional perspectives, attuning your inner vision to enlightenment and abundance. See your third eye fully open and transform into its fifth-dimensional deep glowing green. You now perceive all situations with clarity and insight.

Let this golden light ascend into your crown chakra, clearing and cleansing every aspect of this chakra, activating and energizing it to the fifth-dimensional vibration. The one thousand petaled Lotus of your crown fully opens and glows with a golden light. All your third dimensional chakras are now fully activated and integrated into the 12-chakra system.

All aspects of your third-dimensional Self now aligning to the Mahatma energy, expanding your presence, your awareness and strengthening your connection to all that is. Next, you see this golden light continue to ascend to a space just above and to the back of your head. See the golden light touch and activate your causal chakra. Feel the chakra bursting open and activating your spiritual connection.

Feel your body uplifted as this golden light continues to open and activate your causal chakra, again thanking your Higher Self for assisting you to assimilate this energy. Your causal chakra begins to burn a pure bright white as it elevates your spiritual connection and shields you from drama and negativity.

Imagine that golden light now expanding and activating your soul star chakra, about one foot above your head. See your soul star chakra light up and fully activate, reconnecting you with your wisdom throughout all your incarnations. Feel this connection to Universal wisdom and truth and remember your inherent gifts. See your soul star chakra integrate this golden energy and notice it transforming into a vibrant magenta with hints of blue. Your intentions are now fully supported by your deeper understanding of your self and your soul's purpose.

Imagine the golden light now touches and activates your stellar gateway one meter above your head. See that fifth-dimensional chakra light up and expand like a starburst above you.

Drink in the golden light, blend with the Mahatma energy and thank your Higher Self for helping you assimilate that energy. Notice your stellar gateway is now glowing brightly above you, strengthening your connection to all that is. You now have access to the unlimited light and high-frequency energy of the universe.

Visualize this column of light ascending into the cosmos and connecting with Source, as Mahatma energy continues to flow throughout your activated 12-chakra system, expanding and vibrating within every cell of your body, aligning you to the fifth-dimensional energy. Feel yourself attuned to the fifth- dimensional vibration as your thoughts and intentions ascend to the highest consciousness.

Thank your Higher Self for assisting you in this Attunement and supporting you to realign and fully integrate the Mahatma energy in the perfect way for you.

> Know that you can call upon the Mahatma energy at any time and see the golden column of light radiating from your Merkabah and connecting you into the Earth. See it expanding all around you, beyond the bounds of your body and connecting you to your highest truth.
>
> Take some time to allow the energy to settle and to enjoy the vibrational upgrade. When you are ready, open your eyes and step into your creatorship.

Naomi's story

I worked with Naomi on many occasions over two years. She was a civil engineer working for a private company and she often remarked she was stuck in an 'unfeeling man's world'. Naomi was seeing me for stress and anxiety management, and she was also struggling with IBS. She was very organized, very practical and saw everything as either black or white. The first time I met her she said, "None of that airy-fairy stuff, I just want proper psychology." So, we worked with NLP and positive psychology tools, and she was making progress. I felt like we needed to go a little deeper and I suggested we try hypnosis. She was skeptical, but when she hit a rough patch at work, she thought it was worth a try. During hypnosis, Naomi was able to release significant feelings of anger and resentment that she had carried since she was a teenager.

CHAPTER 7: ASCEND BEYOND NOW – STEPPING INTO THE 12-CHAKRA SYSTEM

After the session, she said she felt better, and she went home. A week later Naomi phoned and told me how much better she felt, how much lighter and happier, and that her IBS symptoms had improved too. She conceded, maybe there was something to this 'weird' stuff, and that she would like to try it again.

We did another hypnosis session and I gave her some simple self-hypnosis techniques to use at home. She loved how easily she could visualize the scenes I guided her through, and she could feel the energy in her body shifting in response to her inner creations. Naomi began doing a simple chakra balancing meditation and was feeling less stressed and her anxiety had all but vanished. She'd stopped taking the 'manliness' of her workplace so seriously and just observed the dynamics and power plays her colleagues always seemed to be involved in. She was in a good place, but she felt she was still not clearly able to see beyond the bravado of her colleagues to understand how she could really make an impact with her work. She recognized her frustration around not 'getting it' at work was exacerbating her IBS symptoms.

I asked her to push herself even further beyond black and white and work through the 12- chakra activation meditation. After the session, Naomi went home, and I didn't hear from her for three months.

Then out of the blue she phoned me. She sounded excited and energized, she sounded like a completely different person. Naomi told me that after our session she had continued to do the meditation to activate her fifth-dimensional chakras. She found herself feeling happy and more in tune each day and began to notice how she saw her colleagues differently. One day she perceived the boss of the company was in a vibration of fear and grief. She felt compelled to ask him if he was okay and he completely opened up to her. He told her he was ill and was trying to figure out who could manage the company in his absence. He had won a new, very lucrative contract but was worried it would not be managed properly without him at the helm.

Naomi was surprised as she hadn't picked up any of this through the banter and bravado of the daily office interactions, but she had noticed other things about her colleagues that she found herself sharing. "Jeff is very discerning and perceptive and always seems to anticipate issues and find the best solutions to mitigate risks. Tom's great with sub-contractors and has a genuine connection with them. They bend over backward to meet deadlines for him. John knows every single cent and every single dollar that has been spent in every budget for all our projects." She just rolled off a list of all the finer attributes of each of her colleagues and talked about the opportunities for improvement with some of their contracts. As she finished her boss was just staring at her. He left the room.

Naomi thought she had put her foot in it, but she had a beautiful vibration in her chest, so she just let it go and went back to work.

As she was leaving that afternoon her boss called her into the office. He told her he wanted her to oversee the company while he took leave and that he was giving her 100% authority to call the shots. He told her about the new contract and said he wanted her to fly to Singapore to meet with the lead agency as soon as possible.

"Why me?" she asked. He told her that the perspective she shared about her colleagues showed a deep level of perception and intuition and that he could see she was passionate about their projects and the interconnected way the team worked together. He said he knew she would make the right decisions for the business and the team because she 'had heart' and would be able to get the best out of them. As you can imagine Naomi was blown away. She was nervous about how her colleagues might react upon finding out she was going to be the boss, but when she told them they all seemed to be relieved. One of them even told her if it had been anyone else, he would have left.

Naomi is now a partner in the business. Her boss is recovering and has seen that he is able to step back and let her lead the way.

THE LEADER WITHIN

The Five Pillars of the Ascension Leadership Model work on the principle of interpromotion to accelerate your personal growth and ascension. You can now see that intuition, transcending current Values Levels of thinking, energetic balance, and having clear intentions are the keys to your success as an ascended leader.

As you are working through the Seven Steps, you will experience significant shifts in your thinking and belief systems and in your energy. I highly recommend you keep a journal or make notes in your diary as you are working through the steps. Continue to record the evidence of your intuition, the guidance you receive and the confirmation of its accuracy. You will always be able to trust it.

As you are resolving Values Levels, make note of the positive learnings or new perspectives you gain as a result of releasing outmoded attitudes. The amount of time it takes to completely work through the Seven Steps is unique to you. Be patient with yourself and take the time you truly need to fully resolve and release those things which no longer serve you.

During the process of clearing and rebalancing your chakras and energy body, you may recall times or situations in your life which once caused you pain or to behave in an unresourceful way. Be gentle with yourself and accept that you were doing the best you could. The purpose of releasing these emotions is not to re-associate into trauma or judge ourselves or others. The butterfly does not resent the caterpillar it once was. Accept and be grateful for all your life experiences and your ability to transcend the aspects which are unsupportive of your purpose.

Be glad of those relationships, hobbies, or even jobs that fall away, be grateful for the lessons they have taught you, and the opportunities they have given you for personal reflection. Being willing to let go or redirect in order to create the best outcomes for all.

This transcendence will inspire your intentions and align you more fully with your purpose. As you create your future, record the date you do the exercise and make notes of the synchronicities that occur to support your outcome. Prepare to be amazed! Even the process of calling in the golden Mahatma energy and activating your 12-chakra system will attract more synchronicities and abundance to you.

Be willing to trust and open to receive. Nothing happens by accident and the Universal energy will align to respond to yours. Nothing is 'fate', it is all alignment.

Be willing to trust and open to receive. Nothing happens by accident and the Universal energy will align to respond to yours.

Though you have been working in the context of leadership throughout the Seven Steps, you will have seen the positive ripple effect this has had on your personal life and you may have uncovered areas of your life where further work is required. Again, be patient and know you have the tools to work through the model as often as you need. Each time you work through the Pillars you will step into a higher energy, with clearer vision and a greater sense of connection.

By now many of these techniques will have begun to integrate into your self-care routine and be a part of your daily or weekly activities. I encourage you to put these techniques into practice in your work as a leader and notice the positive effect you have on those around you.

The Ascension Leadership Model is designed for those who are ready to step up and inspire others. By being in tune with the subtleties of the energy around you and following your intuitive guidance, you are more equipped to respond to any challenge rather than react from the fight or flight of the primitive brain. Others will be uplifted and encouraged by this approach in business and will respond in equally inspiring ways. Why? Because nothing operates in isolation and by liberating the leader within, you are inspiring and assisting others to do the same.

Surround yourself with people who support your personal growth and ascension, those who understand your motivation and are inspired by your purpose. Having someone help you work through challenges can be very beneficial. They can keep you connected to your commitment to finding resolution and assist you to dig a little deeper and go a little further to uncover the parts within you that are ready to be healed and resolved.

> If you would like support when working through the Ascension Leadership Model and access to tools and resources to support the Five Pillars visit *www.theleader-within.com*

I look forward to hearing about your many successes and am optimistic about the positive global shift you are now part of.

It is my honor to share the Ascension Leadership Model with you and to walk with you as you liberate the Leader Within you.

Courtney Jones

GLOSSARY

Ascension – raising to a higher level of energetic vibration, consciousness, spiritual connection, and Values Level thinking.

Attunement - an internal energetic or vibrational shift that allows the body to align with and integrate a new or higher vibration.

Body-mind – the interconnected system of thought, memory and communication residing within the whole body.

Chakra – energy center within the energy body. Often described as a spinning vortex or wheel radiating with color.

Creatorship – your personal ability to create the circumstances in your life. Your ultimate power of creating your desired life experience.

Energy Body – the subtle vibrational component of the body including the etheric body (Aura), emotional body, mental body, spiritual body. The bioenergetic system.

Energetic Vibration – the frequency of the energy body, emotional state or thought patterns. Physical places also hold an energetic vibration which is influenced by the people and events which gather or occur there.

Higher Self – the highest aspect of your consciousness.

Merkabah – a three-dimensional shape of two intersecting tetrahedrons which spin in opposite directions to create an energy field. Considered by some to have a protective purpose and act as a vehicle in which the Soul travels to other dimensions.

Psychophysical – the interconnected relationship between the internal thought process and physical body responses, occurring simultaneously. The physical translation of mental data.

Shift – the movement from one state to another. An up-level in thinking or change in energetic vibration.

Values Level – a lens through which a person views the world, consisting of beliefs, attitudes, thinking and behavioral styles and available internal resources to solve problems.

ACKNOWLEDGMENTS

With love and deepest appreciation to my parents, Bob and Angela, for your unwavering support and belief in me. Seeing you pursue your dreams gives me the strength and courage to follow mine. Thank you for always being there to encourage and guide me, and to offer words of truth and a lens of reality when it really counts.

Love and thanks to Penny and Nick for providing the perfect sibling environment for me to truly understand who I am and to learn the importance of acceptance and flexibility. Thank you for every annoying nickname, resistance to my offers to hypnotize you and your sharp observations of the world.

To my partner Ian, thank you for holding space for me through every step of this journey and continuing to inspire and uplift me. My life is enriched in so many ways through your friendship, love and support – the RPC is thriving!

And to Maggie Wilde, Trish, Carlos, Narelle and the editorial and publishing team at Mind Potential Publishing. Thank you for bringing this book to life.

REFERENCES AND RECOMMENDED READING

Brett, Samantha., and Adams, Steph. *'The Game Changers – Success secrets from inspirational women changing the game and influencing the world.'* ISBN: 9780143787723

Galang, Lufityanto., Donkin, Chris., and Pearson, Joel. *'Measuring intuition: nonconscious emotional information boosts decision accuracy and confidence.'* Psychological science 27.5 (2016): 622-634.

de Vries, Marieke., Holland, Rob W., and Witteman, Cilia L. M. (2008) *'Fitting decisions: Mood and intuitive versus deliberative decision strategies, Cognition and Emotion.'* 22:5, 931-943, DOI: 10.1080/02699930701552580

Graves, Clare W. *'Human Nature Prepares for a Momentous Leap.'*
[From The Futurist, 1974, pp. 72-87. Edited with comments by Edward Cornish, World Future Society.]

Recommended Reading

Beck. Prof Don Edward., Hebo Larsen, Teddy., Solonin, Sergey., Vijoen, Dr Rica., and Johns, Thomas Q. *'Spiral Dynamics in Action – Humanity's Master Code.'* ISBN: 9781119387183

Chopra, Deepak. *'Self Power – Spiritual Solutions to Life's Greatest Challenges.'* ISBN:9781846042874

Lipton, Bruce. *'The Biology of Belief - Unleashing the Power of Consciousness, Matter & Miracles.'* ISBN: 9781401952471

REFERENCES AND RECOMMENDED READING

Gerber, Richard MD., *'Vibrational Medicine – The #1 Handbook of Subtle-Energy Therapies.'* ISBN: 9781879181588

Anodea, Judith PhD. *'Wheels of Life – A User's guide to the Chakra System.'*
ISBN: 97808754232.'03

MEET THE CONTRIBUTORS

Dr Sue Morter

Dr. Sue Morter is an international speaker, Master of Bio-Energetic Theory, and Quantum Field visionary.

She is the *USA Today* #1 bestselling *LA Times* and #1 Amazon bestselling author of:
• The Energy Codes: The 7-Step System to Awaken Your Spirit, Heal Your Body and Live Your Best Life.

The founder and creator of the globally-taught coursework:
• The Energy Codes®, a multi-level body of work on Personal and Spiritual Development

The founder and visionary of:
• Morter Health Center and
• Morter Institute for Bio-Energetics.

She is the creator of:
o   The BodyAwake® RYT 200 Certified Yoga Program and is co-creator of the Bio-Energetic Synchronization Technique (B.E.S.T.).

The host of:
• Gaia TV's *Healing Matrix*, and
• Co-host of *Your Year of Miracles* lifestyle training

www.drsuemorter.com

MEET THE CONTRIBUTORS

This is the full powerful transcript of Dr. Sue's Foreword for this book, *The Leader Within*

"As the world around us continues to change at a rapid rate, the need for Conscious Leadership is greater than ever. The change we are in need of will take courageous women to step up and into their inner wisdom and to embrace their personal power to become ascended leaders.

Throughout my three decades of helping people access their creative wisdom, I have seen more and more evidence of how working with energy and intuition can spark unprecedented personal growth. That step allows leaders to tap into creativity, power, health and compassion to nurture themselves and their relationships. So, too, does it enable them to empower people around them and the community in which they live to activate their potential.

Courtney Jones' **Ascension Leadership Model** *elegantly combines cognitive, energetic and spiritual techniques to provide a strong foundation for creating our life experiences and achieving fulfilment on every level.*

Using high frequency energy patterns, I have worked with people from all walks of life to assist them in elevating their consciousness into life mastery. The Ascension Leadership Model from Courtney Jones speaks closely to an increasingly loud inner calling. The book provides a pathway for coming to know yourself, by unravelling self-imposed limitations that have denied people their true joy and meaning.

Courtney Jones' **Ascension Leadership Model** elegantly combines cognitive, energetic and spiritual techniques to provide a strong foundation for creating our life experiences and achieving fulfilment on every level. The bridge between science and spirituality has been firmly established. Finally, the field of Quantum physics is proving age-old philosophies of energy healing and connectedness with the environment, bringing forward undeniable evidence of the vibrational reality of life. Allopathic health practitioners no longer dismiss energy as a contributing factor to health and healing and are finding more ways to integrate this aspect into their work.

> *work like the* **Ascension Leadership Model** *can proudly take its place as a modern and holistic approach to leadership, personal wellbeing, and selfcare.*

Along with the ground-breaking works by global leaders like Deepak Chopra, Dr. Joe Dispenza, and Dr. Bruce Lipton, my more than 30 years of research and outcomes in the field of energy medicine have helped establish an underlying foundation for additional growth in this exciting field. This, along with the growing body of anecdotal evidence provided by those who have experienced profound personal expansion and healing using energy techniques, means that work like the **Ascension Leadership Model** can proudly take its place as a modern and holistic approach to leadership, personal wellbeing, and selfcare.

- Being joyful and centred in all that you do is a key basis for conscious, ascended leadership and
- By working through the Five Pillars of the Ascension Leadership Model, you will benefit by releasing attachment to negative emotions and letting go of outmoded beliefs and attitudes.
- You will surrender perceived limitations to consciously create the world you want to live in.

It is with gentle guidance and a genuine desire to support your expansion that Courtney passes on her knowledge to enhance cognitive function and mindset, strengthen intuitive connections and energy healing. She takes the reader on a journey to limitless potential, inspiration, and creativity.

The magic of this work is that it benefits all areas of your life and positively influences those around you to step into a higher vibration and ascend into conscious thinking and graceful being.

I am pleased to see Courtney's work offered to the world at a time when it has never been more needed. The Leader Within is an essential, fresh approach to the subject of leadership, there is no doubt this book will empower, uplift, and serve as a catalyst for significant positive change.

Dr. Sue Morter
Founder and CEO of Morter Institute for Bioenergetic Medicine
Author of *The Energy Codes*

The Leader Within is an essential, fresh approach to the subject of leadership, there is no doubt this book will empower, uplift, and serve as a catalyst for significant positive change.

Margot Cairnes
B.Ed. (Hons1), MBA

Margot Cairnes is a pioneer in the field of leadership strategy. She is the author of numerous ground-breaking books including:

- **Peaceful Chaos, The Art of Leadership in Times of Rapid change**
- **Approaching the Corporate Heart**
- **Board Rooms that Work**
- **Staying Sane in a Changing World**

At the core of Margot's work is the compelling connection between a leader's personal inner journey, their ability to drive outstanding levels of corporate success and their capacity to profoundly influence the wellbeing of their wider communities.

While mainly known for her international work with transnationals, Margot also works extensively with emerging entrepreneurs helping them create massive success through understanding the principles of system change and design thinking.

She is highly regarded and respected as an inspirational mentor, advisor and partner to Boards and CEOs of multinational companies.

Margot has twice represented Australia at Women.future.com where she shared the podium with Hilary Clinton and Queen Rania of Jordan in a global webcast out of New York. These forums included a cocktail party on the floor of the New York Stock Exchange where Margot met some of the most powerful women in the world, who gathered to support other women to grow as leader and create a better world for all.

Award winning Australian playwright David Williamson based his play Corporate Vibes on Margot's book "Approaching the Corporate Heart."

The American Biographical Institute calls Margot *"One of the Great Minds of the 21st Century."*

E: margot@margotcairnes.com
W: www.margotcairnes.com

This is the full powerful transcript of Margot's Foreword for this book, *The Leader Within*

"Courtney Jones reminds us of the Dalai Lama's assertion that "The world will be saved by the western woman". The world needs saving.

I am writing this forward in Australia in mid-June 2020. We are not even half way through the year and we have seen the worst drought in 120 years, horrendous bushfires have killed an estimated 1 billion native animals (many which were already on the brink of extinction), we have seen the global economy decimated by COVID-19 lockdown and the death from that virus (at last count) was around 500,000 people. The experts tell us there are more challenges to come.

As I write this, hundreds of thousands of people globally are demonstrating behind the banner of "Black Lives Matter" triggered in the first instance by police brutality against dark skinned people and fueled by endemic racism across the world. Women know that all lives matter.

- The UN tells us that in February 2019 only 24.3 per cent of all national parliamentarians were women and that as of June 2019, only 11 women were serving as a Head of State and only 12 were serving as a Head of Government. As there are 195 countries in the world this means that only 11% of countries have a woman at the helm.

- The figures in the business world are even worse - only 6% of Fortune 500 companies are headed by women!

- The madness we see in climate denial, racial & sexual discrimination, wars, gun violence and domestic violence is mainly being presided over by men.

- Women such as Jacinda Ardern, Prime Minister of New Zealand and Erna Solberg, Prime Minister of Norway show us that leaders can be compassionate, wise and operate from higher level values.

Evolutionary biology tells us that the dominant species is always the slowest to change. It is those who face the most discrimination, the most challenge and feel the most pain who have the greatest incentive to change.

As more and more people suffer from mental illnesses (depression, anxiety, addiction) we hear ever more frequently that it isn't until we hit 'rock bottom' that we are prepared to put in the effort and time involved in personal change. It is personal change that leads to transformation of self, business, community and society in general.

In our highly paternalistic societies, it is women who have the incentive to transform. It is those who transform who will change society for the better.

> This wonderful book, *The Leader Within*, is a workbook, a practical manual for women who want to step up as leaders in our society. It is filled with wonderful tools, insights and models to help you live life to the fullest and bring those about whom you care, along with you on the journey.

I do not know how the society of the future will look. Technological change (hastened by COVID 19 lock down) is changing and will continue to radically change our world.

Yuval Noah Harari in his books, *Homo Deus* and *21 Lessons for the 21st Century*, tells us that we are evolving a new superhuman species – with implanted Artificial Intelligence and Nano Robots who will make, those who can afford it , immortal. The rest of the world (the majority of us) will be "economically irrelevant" because most of the current jobs will be done by robots and AI. By 2029, a $100,000 computer will work better than a human mind. By 2038, it is predicted that we will have human robots. AI doesn't get sick, take holidays or limit its work to an 8 hour day. It doesn't need meal breaks, maternity or compassionate leave. Will humans become irrelevant?

In January 2020 "Millionaires against Pitch Forks' published an open letter in the New York Times pleading with Presidential Candidates to introduce a wealth tax. They claimed that there are 2,153 billionaires in the world who together hold more wealth than 4.6 billion people (that is the same number of people who would make up the entire population of China, India & US combined).

Billionaires and millionaires who include people such as the Disney Family, Warren Buffet, Bill Gates, George Soros and Steven Segel, believe that rising global inequality puts them at risk. They believe that in such an unequal society social unrest (even revolution) is inevitable.

Nick Hanauer, in a webcast, pleaded that although he owned a bank (among other substantial assets) he didn't want to be on the wrong end of a pitchfork should equality lead to social unrest. "Please" he begged "tax the wealthy - including me".

So in the face of rising unemployment, environmental degradation, growing social inequality, increasing mental ill-health and failing medical systems around the world we need a complete transformation.

- Traditional writers tell us that this transformation will come from entrepreneurs

- Women form around 40% of small business owners

- In the face of big data, bio-technology and AI, women will need capital to take their businesses to new levels of influence

- Women have traditionally found it hard to attract capital – especially as their business grows

- Social enterprise will need to play a huge role in working with the world as it changes

- Micro finance (lending small amounts of money to women in the Third World) showed us that when women grow in economic and social power they bring whole villages with them

- We also know that there is an increased link between giving women access to credit and risking them becoming victims of domestic violence.

We need structural change

To get such change we will need to lift our levels of consciousness and subsequently our values.

In this book, *The Leader Within,* Courtney Jones gives us practical tools to grow as human beings; to be more alive, more aware and more purposeful.

If we women want to live in a world of peace, equality, harmony and joy we need to empower ourselves and support our sisters. Using the higher-level values espoused in this book we can then work together to bring our families, our businesses, our society along with us.

Women can save the world.

This book contributes to us becoming the kind of leaders we will need to be to bring about the change that needs to happen."

Margot Cairnes

MEET THE AUTHOR

Courtney Jones

Courtney's initial journey into business and management saw her launching her own successful floristry business in Newcastle, Australia. After selling the business in 2009 she Coached individuals to achieve their life goals.

In 2011 Courtney began working with body language, energy exchange and relationship dynamics; how underlying attitudes effect cohesiveness and ultimately project outcomes. Her exploration sparked a passion for combining energy medicine and its practical implications and implementation into business and leadership.

Alongside her private Leadership Coaching Practice, Courtney continues to work with government and not-for-profit (NFP) organizations on strategic projects. She works closely with Emergency Management Teams in preparedness, planning and implementation during activation for Disaster Responses. Her recent roles include planning and implementation of responses for the 2019 NSW bushfire emergency evacuation centers and response planning in the more recent COVID-19 pandemic.

Courtney brings her unique intuitive leadership approach to her coaching clients today through her studies in Positive Psychology, Modern Hypnosis and Energy Medicine. The development and implementation of her Ascension Leadership Model brings a fresh approach to leadership and business.

MEET THE AUTHOR

COURTNEY JONES
Dip. of Natural Resource Management
Cert. Applied Project Management
Adv. Dip. Applied Hypnotherapy
Dip. NLP and Positive Psychology
Dip. Kinesiology

www.leader-within.com
www.leadershipascensionacademy.com

Download free resources from the book:
www.theleader-within.com

WORKS BY COURTNEY JONES

Books

The Leader Within, The 7 Steps to Ascension Leadership and Intuition in Business

Transformation Journal – Harnessing Energy and Intention for Personal Growth and Transformation

Upcoming Book
Undercover Intuitive- 6 Steps to Strengthen your Intuition to Enhance your Career

Online Courses
Advanced Certificate of Ascension Leadership

Ascension Leadership Coaching Certification
The Undercover Intuitive

Live Seminars and Training
Advanced Certificate of Hypnosis and Trance Healing
Shift and Uplift

CREDITS FOR CHAPTER IMAGES

Introduction
QUOTE
"We think, mistakenly, that success is a result of the amount of time we put in at work, instead of the quality of the time we put in.' Arianna Huffington

Chapter 1: The Ascension Leadership Model
- Kira auf der Heide   instagram.com/kadh.photography

Chapter 2: The Leader Within - Your Intuitive Self
- Conner Bowe

Chapter 3: Where Are You Now – A Baseline for the Ascending Leader
- Daniel Gonzalez   instagram.com/overlyawesome

Chapter 4: Liberate the Leader Within
- Clay Banks   www.buymeacoffee.com/claybanks

Chapter 5: Activate Your Energy Through the Chakra System
- Mark Adriane   markadrianecreative.com

Chapter 6: Your Unlimited Leadership Potential
- Hatham   https://unsplash.com/@hatham

Chapter 7: Ascend Beyond Now – Stepping into the 12 Chakra System
- Mirko Blicke   mirkoblicke.com

The Leader Within
- Evie Shaffer   instagram.com/evieshaffer

WHAT OTHERS HAVE TO SAY

Book Testimonials

"This book throws light on how to achieve true leadership for women to step into their power compassionately and effectively and make the most out of all aspects of their life."

Dr Amanda Hordern, Author of Sex & Cancer
Director Bayside Healthy Living
www.baysidehealthyliving.com.au

....

"I believe this book provides something so unique, something so powerful, something with a feminine energy and a mind-body integrated approach that is not only profound, it is also a must read for anyone who wants to unlock their purpose and step into their power."

Jodi Bradford
Group Experience Manager nib
https://www.linkedin.com/in/jodi-bradford-83654018/

....

"This book gave me hope from the very first chapter, and then delivered on the promise of a straightforward process to access my intuition in business, and not be afraid to use it!"

Kirsten Brumby.
Author of Now What? A Step-by-Step Approach to Land Your New Job or Career, and How to Write Effective Policies and Procedures.
Business Coach and Consultant
www.kirstenbrumby.com

....

"The Leader Within is an essential, fresh approach to the subject of leadership, there is no doubt this book will empower, uplift, and serve as a catalyst for significant positive change."

Dr. Sue Morter
Founder and CEO of the Morter Institute for Bioenergetic Medicine
Author of *The Energy Codes*
www.drsuemorter.com

....

"This book contributes to us becoming the kind of leaders we will need to be to bring about the change that needs to happen."

Margot Cairnes
World-renowned Business Strategist and Author of 4 acclaimed books including: Peaceful Chaos, The Art of Leadership in Times of Rapid change.
www.margotcairnes.com

....

Client testimonials

"It is with caring guidance that Courtney supported me to untangle the blocks and confusion that were stopping me from moving forward. She does this by stretching your understanding and views of the world, gently, to help achieve clarity on the deepest blocks that halt your progress. I love the way she works to keep the momentum going, to not only find your authentic self but to truly love and accept her."

Jodie Esau,
Education Professional and Alternative Health Support.

....

"Over the space of a few weeks, I feel lighter, stronger, and more in control of my journey than ever before. Working with Courtney is a valuable and powerful experience that I would recommend to all."

Lee Baldock, Education Professional.

....

"Courtney not only helped me shift my state of mind and lift me out of my depressed state, she also gave me the tools to help myself."

Simone Kelly, User X Designer.

....

"Courtney is an amazing practitioner, passionate about what she is doing. I had an 8-hour Breakthrough in just one day and I can feel my life changed completely after the session."

Sri Cannon, Positive Energy Psychology Professional.

....

"As an extremely positive, focused, and ambitious woman, a few years ago I found myself a little lost and flat. I started working with Courtney to rediscover my path. Courtney worked alongside me, not preaching, but teaching, opening my mind, heart and eyes to the abundance of possibilities and to get excited about life again."

Sara Martin, Music Industry Manager.

....

www.ingramcontent.com/pod-product-compliance
Lightning Source LLC
Chambersburg PA
CBHW071624080526
44588CB00010B/1257